W9-CHS-695

Beachwalk

An Everyday Journey Through Sea, Sand and Soul

Written and Illustrated by Audrey Schumacher Moe

Walk Publishing

Copylight 2004
All Rights Reserved. No part of this book may be
reproduced or transmitted in any form or by any
means, electrical or mechanical, including photo
copying, recording or by any information storage
and retrieval system, without written consent of the
publisher.

Published by:
Walk Publishing LLC
PO Box 2978
Fallbrook, CA 92088

ISBN: 0-9749885-0-2
Library of Congress Cataloging in Publication Data

for purchase information please contact:
beachwalk@walkpublishing.com

Printed in South Korea
USAsia Press

Written & Illustrated: Audrey Schumacher Moe
Graphic Designer: Orlando Ramos

Beachwalk

An Everyday Journey Through Sea, Sand and Soul.

Walk Publishing

Dedication

Beachwalk is dedicated to all those
who love nature and recognize its importance
in giving meaning and beauty to our lives.

Acknowledgements

In the past, when I read the "I give thanks to" section, it seemed unbelievable so many people could be involved in the undertaking of a book. Now I understand that a book is the result of the input of a great many friends, colleagues, and associates. It is impossible to thank them all, but some stand out. Beachwalk would never have been written were it not for the encouragement of a friend and walking companion, Marilyn Sutton. When my first amateur attempts at writing surfaced, it was Marilyn who read them, saw beyond my first mistakes and pushed me forward. Another walking companion and friend, Doretta Ensign, lent her keen artist's eye to observations of the mysteries of the beach. And Beverly White provided good company and laughter as we walked the sands. Leslie Ernest read some of my early work and gave me tips on writing. Charlie Alexander talked me into taking Jack Grapes Los Angeles writing class, from which I emerged a better writer. A desert friend, Anita Kornfeld, took me into her writing seminar, for which I am grateful. It was an invaluable experience. My desert critique group, Roberta Dinow, Mel Benjamin, Joanna Jacobs, Mary Olson, Gordon Gumpertz, listened faithfully to each chapter of Beachwalk and gave me good advice. Rachel Druten invited me to her critique group with Barbara Seranella where my writing was validated. The Original Palm Springs Writers Guild has been a inspiration with monthly meetings featuring successful writers who shared their expertise. I thank Richard Soltys, who introduced me to USAsia Press and Orlando Ramos who designed the book.

My son, Carter Moe, my two daughters, Heather Moe, a writer, and Holly Moe, an artist, always urged me forward with encouraging words. Most of all I thank my husband, Courtney Moe, who gave up so much so I could write and do the paintings for this book.

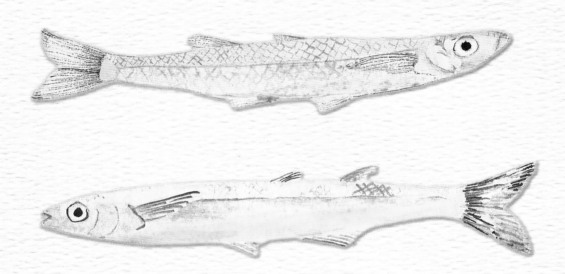

Grunion, *Leuresthes tenuis,* a type of smelt about 6 inches long. Only fish in the world to spawn on land. In the Spring,
they swim onto the beach, lay and fertilize their eggs and return to sea on the wash of the next wave. Grunion hunting,
a California tradition, takes place on spawning nights when the fish may be gathered by hand, roasted and eaten.

LOS ANGELES

NEWPORT BEACH

CRYSTAL COVE STATE PARK
LAGUNA BEACH

DANA POINT

ISTHMUS

AVALON

SANTA CATALINA
ISLAND

SAN DIEGO

Preface

This book grew over twenty years of daily roamings along a strand of lightly traveled California coastline. Bordered on the north by Newport Beach and the small coastal village of Corona del Mar and on the south by Laguna Beach, Crystal Cove State Park includes over 3 miles of ocean front. I first knew the area as Horse Beach, an informal name used by locals because of the stable on the bluff top. Later when the land was purchased for a state park, it officially became Crystal Cove State Park.

As I returned from my walk each morning, renewed and ready for the day ahead, I felt drawn to my brushes and journal, eager to record the moments I valued. These excursions on the beach evolved into meaningful interludes of reflection on the life I had followed through marriage, child raising and finally leisure time for projects of my choice. Gradually these moments built one upon the other, casting their hues over my mental palette as well as my paintings.

As the beach changed, so did I. While I loved sunny days, I also learned to appreciate misty fog-filled mornings from which some of my most soul touching experiences emerged. Participating in each day's adventure with its movement from tide line to relationships, rocky ledges to challenges, churning sea to fresh opportunity, spun a story so rich and varied I needed not only to record it, but to share it with all who would walk with me. I invite you on my coastal beachwalks, my small journeys of discovery. They have served me well in navigating the turns of life. May they provide a gentle companion for your journey.

X

Introduction

I was four years old when my mother died. She was thirty four and left nine children, four boys and five girls, the youngest of which were my six month old twin sisters. I recall very little from that time. My most vivid memory is from my mother's funeral. I can still see my father and my eight siblings sitting in a small side room on chairs lined up in two rows. Heavy closed draperies separated us from the people in the big room. I had no idea what was going on, but I knew for sure it was bad, because my father was crying. That year when my mother left this world, I began my life with an elderly great Auntie, who raised me as if I were her own.

From that beginning in rural Minnesota, the woods, lakes and plains of middle North America, I ended up forty-three years later on the very western edge of the continent in a house facing the infinite sea. A house from which each evening a fire ball sun drowned in the ocean leaving behind a sky layered with orange, red, cerise, and mauve. Each morning an ever changing horizon of waves and fog and glimpses of offshore islands once attached to the land beckoned me with beguiling promises.

All was new in this world I had not known as a child. Every excursion on the beach uncovered mysteries, creatures to identify, names to memorize, life cycles to follow. Corona del Mar and Crystal Cove State Beach, part of the California coastline midway between Los Angeles and San Diego were my hunting grounds, my text for learning. So I began my beachwalks, walks that soon taught me to appreciate the butterfly and crab, the fog and mist as well as the sun and diving dolphins. A grain of sand might hold my interest and help me see life in perspective just as much as the sight of a breaching whale.

Local surfers called it Horse Beach. Because of its seclusion and long stretches of breaking surf, it was an ideal place to catch the waves. On this stretch of pristine sand, favorite coves were marked with whimsical driftwood shelters offering some protection from sun and wind, but mostly representing a collective surfing comradeship. Only the adventurous crawled through the fence on the highway above, hiked across open fields and slipped down steep cliffs to reach the beach below.

There were always a few beach parties, on weekends a sprinkling of day visitors, and once in a while, a vagrant would spend the night under the stars next to the surf. But most of the time the beach was deserted, the domain of birds, sea lions and a myriad of small sea creatures. Residents of Cameo Shores, a small community to the north and where I live, held coveted keys to a locked gate allowing use of the secluded beach. The land was privately owned and had not changed significantly since the time when early explorers trekked through California territory with hopes of colonizing the New World.

At Crystal Cove, a midpoint in the three mile stretch of beach, forty-two vintage cottages look out to sea from their cliff-side perches. Hidden from the highway by trees and brush, some are tucked in along a drainage stream from the hills beyond. These cozy seaside dwellings provide a comforting presence of others, who love the solitude and spiritual qualities of relatively untouched coastal shoreline.

Once a boarding stable sat on the bluff above the shoreline. Its trails led across the coastal terrace through fields of wild sage and buckwheat and finally to steep, rock-studded paths snaking down gnarled cliffs of faulted sandstone to waves and beach below. My first visits to this wild, isolated environment were imprinted with the image of a horse and rider galloping along on hard-packed sand by the water's edge. In my mind, I can still see the horse stumbling as an unpredictable wave pushes higher on the beach. Regaining its footing, horse and rider head away from the surf to safer ground.

The stable is long gone now and only jutting crags of sea-washed rock form images as misty blue-gray waves toss their sparkle upon the shore. Where horses once grazed, brushy Deerweed and tiny Sun Cup compete for space amongst alien Wild Mustard and Tree Tobacco. Small animals rabbits, ground squirrels, skunks, rodents and reptiles shelter under stands of saltbush and the melodious song of the Meadowlark mingles with the soft mewing of the California Gnatcatcher.

This undeveloped piece of ground and seacoast became my hideaway and my renewal as I discovered its treasures through daily excursions. The soft beach sand became my jogging path, the sea life cast upon the shore my textbook. Each day's variations stimulated my desire to learn. As time passed my knees stiffened and the jogs became walks. The beach went through adjustments as well. On the bluff top development plans were proposed but later revised as the beach and inland area were designated a state park. At first little changed, but then herb-scented paths gave way to a golf course and elaborate Mediterranean villas filled the fields between my home and the park. Where before I had walked wild trails, my gate led instead to asphalt golf cart paths, and the spice of natural sage mingles with the scent of newly mown grass. Horse Beach is now Crystal Cove State Park and with public access has come parking lots, paved trails, and public restrooms. The vintage beach cottages at Crystal Cove have been vacated and more changes are to come.

I still love this beach and it remains my refuge and place of renewal, and now I share it with others who can find healing in the sand and sea. Of those who visit this beautiful strip of coastline, few will know or remember its history as Horse Beach, let alone recall scenes with horses picturesquely poised atop the bluff or at the water's edge. For me, I like to think that on a foggy morning, if I squint my eyes, I can just make out the shape of a horse and rider melting into the foamy surf. But when I blink, all that is left is misty air; the figures fade from sight, but not from memory.

I was fortunate to experience Horse Beach at a special time in history, a time when this small section of California coastline was still wild and sparsely populated. Yet as things change I must accept what change brings. My beachwalks changed me, they enriched and shaped my life. I invite you to join me on these walks and through my discoveries find your life changed, as you think about the treasures each of us can find, if only we take time to look.

Chapters

Beachwalk
a time for contemplation

*"I think that I cannot preserve my health and spirits,
unless I spend four hours a day at least...sauntering
through woods and over hills and fields, absolutely free
from all worldly engagements."*

Henry David Thoreau

A friend once told me Africa was a place that transformed him into a spiritual being. His experiences there were so meaningful he felt at peace and content. Africa was his beachwalk. My beachwalk developed while actually walking the beach. But now I know a beachwalk can be anywhere. It need only be a time alone, a way of seeing through eyes wider than the narrow slits of daily routine, a transcendence to a broader concept of self and environment. By eliminating ordinary distractions and seeing my surroundings with a clear and open mind, a deeper level of value assessment is possible and new realizations rise to the surface of my thinking.

On my beachwalk this morning I sit absorbing the moisture and the moment as I filter tiny grains of shiny quartz sand through my fingers. The salt of the sea rubs off and sticks to my hand, leaving a residue I try to brush off on my jacket. But my fingers continue to feel damp and I realize I can't brush off the sea. It clings to me with a magnetism that heals as it pulls me close and seeps into my inner being. When I first began walking the beach, I did not know there is a healing the sea brings. It rolls in with every breaking wave, spraying its spirit upon the shore in misty droplets and hangs suspended, waiting to be inhaled by any willing wanderer. Like the laying on of hands, it has power for those who embrace it.

My first times spent on this wild, deserted beach were adventures so new to me I could only appreciate a sense of being here, recognizing I was ignorant of most of its aspects. Every shell, plant and bit of sea life was a mystery to me, but something I wanted to know about. So for my own satisfaction, I began to research and collect information. As time went by and I learned about the sea and the mysteries offered up on its sandy, rocky shore, I was surprised to find I was learning about myself as well. And this is how my concept of beachwalk came into being.

Once I learned to beachwalk at the beach, I found I could beachwalk wherever I might be. In the Spring when I spend several months in the local mountains, I take my beachwalk on rocky trails lined with red-stemmed Manzanita and tall, hundred year old Jeffrey Pines. Mountain Blue Jays scold and gray squirrels chatter in tree tops. Sometimes I just walk around the neighborhood enjoying the tulips, iris and lilacs blooming in mountain gardens.

One year on a summer trip to Wisconsin to visit my husband's parents I took my beachwalk in the afternoon at a small lake. Instead of walking, I sat on the edge of a gently rocking dock, alternately peering into quiet water hoping to catch a glimpse of life beneath the surface, while savoring every word and watercolor drawing in *The Country Diary of an Edwardian Lady* by Edith Holden. She made her first entry on January 1, 1909 and continued for a year to record the countryside surrounding her village in Warwickshire, England. I feel certain her observation of nature served as her beachwalk and added to mine. I wish she could have known the pleasure her journal has given to another woman on another continent nearly a hundred years later.

As I feed my body and take care of it physically, I also make time for my beachwalk to feed my soul. Resting from the usual makes it possible for me to return to the usual and tackle ordinary and unpleasant tasks with renewed enthusiasm. I see my beachwalk not as a treat, but as a necessity. While I recognize not everyone can beachwalk at the beach, most can find some small bit of quiet time alone, when all that is buzzing around in the brain is swept aside and for a brief time peace and serenity have a chance to reign. Thus the spirit is renewed and prepared to face the tribulations of everyday life.

I compare my beachwalk to the cleansing incoming tide. It sweeps away yesterday and leaves me with a clean slate. It helps me look at my world as fresh and shiny, like wet pebbles with all their beauty enhanced by a film of fresh sea water. It reminds me I do not have to walk in yesterday's footprints. I can make my own anew and aim them where I please.

Finally the dampness in the sand where I'm sitting soaks through the seat of my cotton sweat pants and I get up to continue my beachwalk. As I wander happily along the wave line oblivious to anything except the tranquil moments I'm experiencing, time stops, my mind is at rest, and I am free and ready for more lessons from the sea.

Three-Winged Rock Shell, *Pterynotus trialatus*. An attractive rock shell found from California to Mexico. Bizarre and decorative varieties of its family, Muricidae exist in tropical seas.

When I arrive home chilled from my damp clothes and the fog that's beginning to roll in, I am still wrapped in a blanket of renewal from the power of the sea on my thinking. I see the day ahead as full of pleasant options and anything is possible.

Tide Pools
the missing octopus

"All things---linked are,"
"That thou canst not stir a flower,
Without troubling of a star."

Francis Thompson

It is January 1st, New Year's Day. While most people are watching football bowl games, I prefer to spend the afternoon at the beach checking out tide pools. An exceptionally low tide has left a wide expanse of uneven sand and rocky basins filled with sea water, a perfect invitation for observation of intertidal dwellers hidden in nooks amidst seaweed and algae covered rocks. Clumps of surf grass, ordinarily undulating back and forth with each wave surge, now lie flat upon the sea-sculpted, rock layer separating sandy beach from deeper water off shore. Missing is the vibrant, pulsating sound of booming waves; there is no ebb and flow of swirling sea water from the surf. Instead, a stillness prevails. The beach is transformed into a quiet garden of shallow pools filled with intertidal sea life.

As I pick my way over slippery, algae-covered rocks peppered with tiny Periwinkle Snails, I try to avoid crushing them with my feet while making my way seaward. But their abundance defeats my efforts. I pause and crouch down to watch Turban Snail shells inhabited by Hermit Crabs move slowly across the bottom of a pool, leaving wiggly trails in the sand. A brief silver flash catches the corner of my eye as an Opaleye, alerted by my shadow crossing its pool, scurries for cover. I sit quietly and wait until this minnow-sized fish, sensing no movement above, feels safe enough to leave its hiding place and swim confidently around.

From a thin crack between two moss covered rocks, I pry out a three inch, Purple-hinged Pecten shell, *Hinnites multirugosus,* both halves still intact and connected, but the shell is empty of the living mollusk. When alive, it swims in what we would call a backwards direction, by flapping together the two halves of its shell. It lives in deeper water, so when this one died, it was carried shoreward where waves wedged it into a rock crevice.

A few times I have been lucky enough to find a *Modiolus capax* or Fat Horse Mussel washed up on the sand. Most of our California coast mollusks are small and drab colored to blend with the pebbles and seaweed found on our rugged, wave-scoured shores. But the Fat Horse Mussel has a deep pink, almost red colored shell which it disguises with a brown periostracum or outer covering. The shell's drab exterior reminds me of people who construct a similar disguise, hiding a beautiful, colorful layer underneath their less attractive outward appearance. Many times I have used a first impression to judge character and then found out I was wrong. Inner beauty is seldom worn on the surface like a coat, but tends, instead, to be the dress underneath revealed only after a shedding of the outer layer. One of my best friends is a quiet person I took no interest in when first introduced. Later on I discovered how much we had in common and how comfortable it is to be with her. We have since gone on many trips together and I know I can always count on her. Our personalities are so completely different we never compete, instead we complement each other.

Further out I spot a bed of Green Sea Anemones under a rocky ledge. Their pale turquoise and gray-green tentacles wave gently like flags in the breeze as they gather food from the water around them. Beyond the anemones, sea urchins, each a ball of purple spikes, nestle into individually sized nooks scraped into the stone. chitons, prehistoric creatures with a shell consisting of a series of plates joined together like armor, dot the rocks. Their ancestors lived on earth during the time of the dinosaurs.

Giant Rock Scallop, *Hinnites multirogosus.*

Like Sea Urchins they survive pounding surf by adhering tightly to a solid boulder. They make me think of suction cups; once fastened down, it is almost impossible to pry them away from their spot. Again, I am reminded of how people find their own niches and hold on, sometimes displaying superhuman strength to survive hard times, especially during times of crisis.

Out beyond the Sea Anemones I begin to see large clumps of Blue Mussels covering the ocean side of many intertidal rock outcroppings. Densely packed and piled on top of each other, they are one of the most common mollusks of the beach. So prolific are they, I sometimes neglect to appreciate their beauty until bits of broken blue shell flash indigo in the sand and remind me. One year after a storm, so many were dislodged and thrown in piles upon the shore their stench, as they rotted in the sun, became almost unbearable. Residents living above the beach were forced to move out for several weeks, illustrating the power of numbers. A few dead mussels smell bad, but multitudes overwhelm.

Someone calls out they have found a Starfish, so I wander over to see it. Sea Star is a better name for this orange, five armed creature, since it is certainly not a fish. But more importantly, at least there is one today. Not too many years ago, Sea Stars were abundant. Now when only one or two can be found, each is a treat.

Purple Sea Urchin, *Strongylocentrotus purpuratus*. One of the best known species in the world. The hard shell without spines is called a test.

Back in my early beachwalking days, I once saw an octopus in a seaweed covered tide pool. As it waved two of its tentacles in the weed, I watched them change color from light tan matching the bottom sand to the greenish gray of the floating seaweed. It made me aware of how people also change to match their environment. Think city people and country folk. Most of us are constantly trying to fit in. Why else do we buy new clothing each year as styles change when last year's outfits are perfectly good.

Inner surface of Giant Rock Scallop. Note rich purple color at hinge.

No one finds an octopus in the tide pools today. It worries me that tide pool life has noticeably diminished in the years I've been experiencing the beach. I am well aware marine environments change as scarcity and abundance trade places, always trying to strike a balance. Even the lowliest of sea creatures has been known to migrate. A researcher reporting in *Natural History* magazine in 1994 presents evidence that a significant migration of Acorn Barnacles, mussels, Periwinkles, Sea Urchins, and Sea Stars occurred from the North Pacific to the North Atlantic, most likely through the Bering Strait. Thirty-three percent of the 335 shell-bearing species living between southern Labrador and Cape Cod, Massachusetts can have their origins traced to the North Pacific. None of this happened overnight. For example, the common Periwinkle and most abundant mollusk on rocky shores from Newfoundland to New York, is closely related to a fossil species from California dating back 2.4 million years.

So changes I've seen in the twenty years of my beach experience are nothing in the geological time scale. However, what effect of which we are not yet aware, will tide pool depletion have on other things? The interconnectedness and dependency of all living beings is so intricate and subtle that we often cannot know all of its secrets until the damage is done.

I look around at the other beachgoers today, who have come here to observe tide pool life and I wonder about our impact as we move about trampling on fragile sea life. We mean no harm. But every footstep on the Acorn Barnacle and Periwinkle covered rocks crushes life, leaving the dead where live creatures once dwelled. Yet, how do we appreciate and learn to love these creatures if we cannot see them in their natural environments? Once again I see the power of numbers, a few people looking at tide pools is tolerable; many over time become destructive and upset the balance.

As I walk, I realize the tide pools are a text for life, a balanced community inhabited by predator and prey. Each shell and living creature reminds me in some way of human behavior I can relate to. The tenacity of the Chitons, the Hermit Crab's change of home as it grows, the Fat Horse Mussel's dull outer cover up, all correspond to human traits. So as I study the tidepools, I study my own behavior as well. The importance of balance in a tide pool community is similar to that of a human community. It gives me a goal to strive for. I must be careful not to insist upon what I want, but to strive for balance.

In today's world, invasion and extinction are occurring on a daily basis and the consequences are not as yet definitive. Water quality in general is deteriorating along our coast, so the presence of the Green Sea Anemones I see today is hopeful, since they do not tolerate pollution and thus are an indicator of clean water in this locale.

Comparing species comings and goings on a geological time scale may present some clues for today's events, if we consider the past as a key to the present and a possible guide to the future. I don't think I'll worry much about the next million years, but certainly there are considerations that need looking at now.

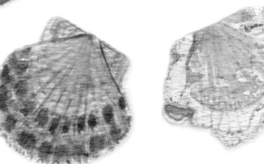

Giant Rock Scallops in various stages of growth. They begin life as free-swimming scallops, but later on attach to stationary object.

Fat Horse Mussel, *Modiolus capax*, found from Santa Cruz, California to Peru. Most of the chestnut-brown periostracum or outer covering has peeled off these shells revealing the deep pink coloring underneath.

As I continue thinking about how much the tide pools tell me, I notice the sun is low in the western sky. Slanted rays bounce off the water, making it difficult to see through the glare and I realize it is time to leave my tide pool textbook. Tomorrow is a new day and if I come back another time at low tide, maybe I'll see an octopus.

Tide pool Wooly Sculpin, *Clinocottus analis australis*, spends its whole life in tide pools.
Found dead on the beach, I stored this fish in my freezer until I had time to paint it.

Dolphins
rescuers of the sea

"The earth does not belong to us,
we belong to the earth."
Chief Seattle

Dolphins! Close to shore, just beyond the breaking surf, black fins on curved dark backs slice gracefully through gray-green water, tilt forward and roll back into the sea. From my vantage point on the beach, I scan the horizon, waiting the few seconds it takes for the fins to reappear and repeat their graceful water ballet, a rhythmic motion of dorsal fins surfacing and gliding, disappearing and resurfacing.

I saw them the first time, soon after my husband and I moved our family from the hills around Los Angeles to the coast where I began taking exercise walks on the beach. The appearance of the dolphins one morning caught me by surprise. I had no idea they came so close to shore. Breathless and still, I watched with wonder as a small pod moved leisurely down the coast just beyond the breaking surf. Wanting to keep even with them, I hurried along, savoring each brief glimpse of their sleek bodies cutting through the waves. They were so near I felt a part of their world and claimed them as a part of mine. With the dolphins so close, I gained a sense of belonging, as if this new place had opened its doors and invited me in. I've seen them many times since, but the thrill of that first sighting remains.

There are probably no more then six or eight in the group I watch today. Other times, I have seen as many as fifty or more,

Mother and baby dolphin,
Tursiops truncatus, the West Coast dolphin.

rolling and leaping as if at play, and those were only the fins I could count. These are our resident Bottlenose Dolphins, *Tursiops truncatus.* They live and function together as a family while cruising the Southern California coast in search of feeding grounds.

I once read about six dolphins in Santa Monica Bay, who surrounded a weakened young female, keeping her afloat. A conservation group stood by observing for ten days. "As long as the family is with her, there is no need for intervention," they said. "They'll keep shepherding her along so long as she needs help." I love this story as an example of how these intelligent mammals care for one another.

Legends run through world history of dolphins rescuing people at sea by holding an injured or exhausted person above water. We have our own dolphin rescue story that occurred at San Clemente, south of Crystal Cove Beach. A surfer, in search of better waves, had paddled down coast from his two buddies when a big wave caught him off balance and he fell, hitting his head on his board. Unconscious and unnoticed, he lay face down in the water. That was when observers witnessing the accident from the bluff above saw dolphin fins surround him.

Astonished, they watched the dolphins move in and turn over the limp, still form as they rode their bodies under him for support. The amazed observers scrambled down the bluff shouting for help. When the other two surfers were alerted and finally reached their buddy, he was alive because of the dolphins. So the stories are true.

History confirms the presence of a physical and mystical bond between us and the dolphins. I think of the leaping dolphin frescoes in the palace of Knossos on the island of Crete and ancient Greek coins etched with boys riding dolphins. They picture the magic I feel on mornings when I see dolphins in the ocean close to shore and near me.

Dolphins are so like us. As air breathing mammals they can drown just as we can, they have the same body temperature as we do, they live in family groups and bear their young live. Above all, they are very intelligent. At one time, with Earthwatch in Hawaii, I participated for several weeks in a dolphin study where I watched daily as two captive dolphins showed their understanding of our language by responding to hand gestures and underwater sounds. In one example, when given the words, "fetch, hoop, ball," with gestures, they retrieved the ball and put it through the hoop. If only we could understand and know the meaning of the clicks and sounds of their language. Then we could know what they would like from us.

Now I watch dolphins from the beach. From twenty-year studies conducted by local experts, I learn the identified resident pod numbers about 800. But how are they faring? Toxins and poisons from contaminated water reach dolphins through fish they eat, just as we are affected by eating unsafe sea food. While the ocean water can absorb and cleanse many contaminants caused by human activity, there is a saturation point we need to know about before we have polluted to a point of no return. We are depending upon the dolphins to serve as our early warning signal of ocean health. Dolphins have saved individuals, but can they rescue civilization from drowning in its own created waste?

When I see them this morning, I am delighted to catch a glimpse of my ocean friends and find myself overwhelmed as usual by their graceful beauty. But most of all I am happy to know they are still there, and as I watch them roll on, I feel safe.

Siver
CA. 344 B.C.

Ancient coins depict humans riding dolphins. Dolphins and man have had a mystical connection throughout history.

Roman coin
CA. 74 B.C.

Why, I wonder, do dolphins rescue people? Is this their natural instinct learned from pushing their own newly born to the surface to breathe? Or is it a kind of mutual attraction between man and dolphin we simply don't yet understand?

Wild Fields

a perfect world

"What is this life if, full of care,
We have no time to stop and stare?"

William Henry Davies

Some mornings I drive to the gym to exercise my body, but mornings like this, when I walk the paths to the beach, I nourish my soul. The moment I remove the woven lanyard and key from around my neck to unlock the metal mesh gate between my street and the coastal terrace above the beach, I step into another world. This is my entry to wild fields of herb-scented sage and buckwheat, to masses of yellow-rayed Encelia, to stands of invasive Artichoke Thistles thrusting round purple shaving brush heads upward to the sun. It is, as well, my entry into another frame of mind, one marked by serenity and a sense of well being, but sparked with anticipation of discovery.

I gaze ahead at mounds of saltbush rising above the silvery sheen of pale green and white grass seed heads swaying rhythmically in gentle waves. Lavender Storksbill and white Popcorn Flowers line sandy pathways polka-dotted with paw prints left by rabbits on their early morning forage. A Red-tailed Hawk hovers in an updraft. Wings stationary, it rides the wind from the sea as it ascends steep sandstone cliffs bordering the beach. Only the slightest movement of its wing tips is needed to keep it aloft. Near the ground, small white Cabbageworm Butterflies flit delicately around sweet scented native plants as the hum of bees in the Wild Mustard creates a soothing background like soft stringed music. The pristine, untamed scene before me calms my mind and penetrates deeply into my inner being, pushing out crowded unsettling thoughts milling around inside my head. My heart and mind are cleansed and ready for today.

It is during moments like this, when the small world around me seems so absolutely perfect, that I feel empowered and strong. In this temporary Eden, I too, am momentarily perfect and content. I desire nothing more than that which exists at this minute in time. One thing I have learned from nature is to give in to the moment, to savor its sensory nuances. Nature at its best is always right, complete, perfect. Each rock, plant, cliff, or small creature belongs. Nothing is out of place where man treads lightly with no need to embellish or destroy what nature has created.

Each morning as I inhale the view along with the pervasive scent of wildness emanating from pores of plants and roots hugging the soil, I am filled with a sense of peacefulness. I become a time traveler exploring a new world. It is my interlude between sleep and work when I experience the fields and the beach. It is my time away, my beachwalk. Not that I want to stay permanently in my idealized world of nature; I just want to drop in for a short daily visit to soak up the healing spirit of things that grow and live unattended. After every small excursion into that world, I return home infused with strength, renewed and ready.

If everyone could have a beachwalk, wherever they may be, I believe the world would be a gentler place. Experiencing peace and quiet for a short time removes the need for aggression against our neighbors by combating the stresses built up from difficulties encountered in our daily lives. When water in a tea kettle gets hot, pressure is relieved through steam

Sea Rocket, *Cakile edentula,* a member of the Mustard family, named for the rocket-like shape of the seed pods. The young stems and leaves have a pungent taste somewhat like horseradish.

Long-beaked Storksbill, *Erodium botrys,* from the Geranium family.
Dry, spiral shaped seedbeaks are carried by the wind for seed distribution.

leaving the open spout. Whereas a tightly closed pressure cooker with no outlet can explode if not gauged properly. A regular beachwalk relieves pressure, allows it to escape like steam and avoids exposive emotions.

We are so geared to our fast paced world, serenity does not come naturally.

I find by making time for moments alone to think on my own without the blare of radios and television or traffic and city noise, I can keep my spirit alive. I don't have to be trapped into following the ideas of others thrown at me from media sources. Not that I don't listen to the radio, TV or read newspapers, it's that I balance them with a beachwalk.

I don't expect to always have the beach available for my beachwalk. When the day comes for me to move from my home near the water, I will take my beachwalk elsewhere, in the desert, country, suburbia, or city street, but I will still be beachwalking and searching for the interesting and best in my surroundings. I will still be providing an outlet for the steam of stress.

For now the beach remains my outlet. My walks and my thoughts are recorded for those who would join me in my attempt to understand more, learn about the world around me through observations and small discoveries and to therefore live better. I pick a stem of Storksbill with its purple flowers and carry it carefully home to place in a glass of water until I have time to set out paper and paints to record this small thing, this interesting thing, this discovery from my morning beachwalk.

Ice Plant, *Mesembryanthemum crysstallium*, was introduced to North America from southern Europe and Africa. Little beads on the stems are swollen with water and give the plant a moist feel and icey look.

Scaly Worm Tubes

an unwelcome gift

"It is not what you have lost, but what you have left that counts."

Harold Russell

Scaly worm tubes litter the morning beach. Dislodged by heavy storm waves from the safety of colonies wedged between rocks and narrow crevices, they lie scattered upon the shore in bits and pieces. Some are in clumps entwined so tightly they form an inseparable mass, while others are single, elongated, twisted, contorted tubes. No two are alike, each is distinct in its growth pattern and its own particular beauty.

As I examine a handful of these empty shells, the variety of twisted, distorted shapes makes me think of meandering paths and turbulent events. They remind me of a time when my life was as twisted and unsure as the most distorted mass of scaly worm tubes. It was just after the diagnosis: a malignant tumor - breast cancer. At that moment, my life as I knew it ceased to exist. I was emptied of my previous reality and tossed into a void of disbelief and fear.

My world suddenly became distorted and twisted as I gathered information and agonized over choosing the right doctors and types of treatment. Staying alive became the objective of each day. And lurking in the background was always the thought of how I would approach death with dignity and courage, should that become my only option.

Painfully, I worked through the decisions, a lumpectomy, and a second operation removing lymph nodes to see if the cancer had spread. Since test results showed the diseased cells had begun their relentless march to overtake my body, the next steps were radiation and chemotherapy. Those were the most difficult days. Hours spent in the doctor's office, needle in my arm, the I.V. dripping its healing poison into my bloodstream and the recognition that just as I began to feel better, it would all begin again. Life came in short straight spurts and long twisting detours.

During this time, I didn't get to the beach. Some days, just walking from one end of the house to the other took an enormous effort. When I think about it now, even though I used meditation tapes and positive thinking, I wish I had pushed myself and gone on short beachwalks. I needed the healing of ocean and sand and salt air.

Nearly a year passed. Finally the treatments ended and I returned to my "normal life." But my normal life was gone. Gone was the year, and lost was my sense of youthful immortality. So it could happen to me! My new vulnerability brought with it a heightened awareness, a sensitivity and an appreciation of the commonplace, the simplest of moments.

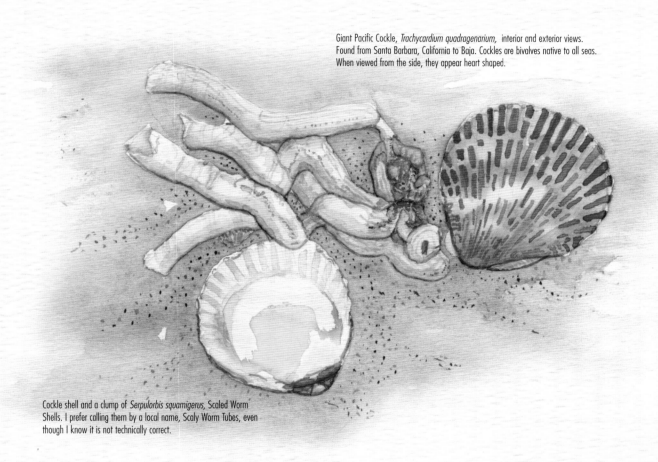

Giant Pacific Cockle, *Trachycardium quadragenarium*, interior and exterior views.
Found from Santa Barbara, California to Baja. Cockles are bivalves native to all seas.
When viewed from the side, they appear heart shaped.

Cockle shell and a clump of *Serpulorbis squamigerus*, Scaled Worm
Shells. I prefer calling them by a local name, Scaly Worm Tubes, even
though I know it is not technically correct.

Today my experience with cancer is but a vague memory. The physical pain and sickness I suffered are long gone, but the fear and depression inherent in a life threatening disease I still recall vividly. I learned how a negative situation can turn into a positive influence, as I look at the world differently now, knowing all any of us has is the moment we are experiencing. Our ultimate power is how we choose to live that moment.

The gift of scaly worm tubes scattered over the sand this morning helps me remember bad times have value with lessons to be learned that can become a foundation for good times. I see truth and beauty in the scaly worm tubes I hold in my hand and I choose the most distorted clump to take home with me as a reminder.

Waves
tsunamis of change

*"The ultimate measure of a person is not where they stand
in moments of comfort and convenience,
but where they stand in times of challenge and controversy."*

Dr. Martin Luther King, Jr

My beachwalk this morning is on the bluff top instead of down on the sand. If I had checked my tide table before I left home, I would have known an extra high tide covers the beach at this hour. Most days sand extends from cliff side to between fifty and a hundred feet or more before meeting the surf. But today waves roll all the way to the foot of the bluff, splashing upward and bouncing back to meet the next incoming breaker. Since I can't be down on the sand, I decide to enjoy a view of the water from above.

As I look out to sea at white-capped waves thrashing their way shoreward, my attention focuses on one long wave stretching along the entire coast within my view. Usually waves come in sets of many short breakers hitting the beach obliquely at different intervals. I follow the direction of this long wall of water heading towards shore and watch it dissolve into the sand of the beach. The next wave also stretches along the shoreline as far as I can see. Each new wave conforms to the same pattern and I begin to wonder why I have never before paid much attention to the waves, other than appreciating their intrinsic beauty.

When I first began walking the beach, waves were a dominant element contributing to the atmosphere of my beachwalk, thundering their presence and spraying their spittle into the air, but they were secondary to my experiences on land. I liked it best when the tide was out leaving lots of sand and space to explore. Until today I really didn't notice wave patterns, how they hit the beach in sets, nor did I think about waves as a part of my beach education. I was too busy searching for shells, learning the names of shorebirds and puzzling over unfamiliar sea life stranded on the sand. I left the waves to the surfers.

crab carapace inside

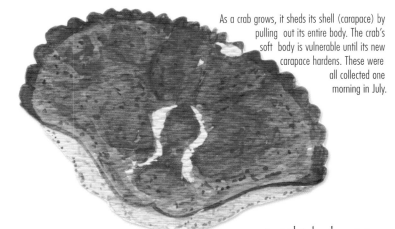

As a crab grows, it sheds its shell (carapace) by pulling out its entire body. The crab's soft body is vulnerable until its new carapace hardens. These were all collected one morning in July.

As I think about it now, I realize I was living the same way, looking for newness and giving little attention or appreciation to the ordinary around me. I was going through life accepting the waves of change, focused on ripples instead of whole waves. Looking back, I see I often barely recognized each new wave as it came splashing over me. Getting through each day as I tried to fulfill my sense of duty as wife, mother and friend propelled me forward in my personal sea. I didn't question the waves or wonder where they came from, I just rode them. At the time they seemed regular and normal, as I splashed happily on through each day without a lot of questioning.

Many of my life waves were like the soft rolling ocean wave I love for playing in the surf. It breaks far enough out and with enough strength to give me an exciting ride in to shore on my little Styrofoam kickboard without putting me in any significant danger. Concentrating to catch a wave just right, feeling the stimulation of foaming salt water splashing over my body, and

veined rock

38

enjoying the exhilarating ride, all are so much fun, I don't notice the cold water. I can stay in for hours and still find it hard to drag myself out when I know I must. Much of my life has been made up of these soft rolling waves that provide stimulation and gentle fun, while helping me overlook petty annoyances.

But not all waves are so gentle. In the ocean, tsunamis or tidal waves can be as much as a hundred feet high and pack unbelievable power. In Papua, New Guinea, a tsunami only thirty feet high hit a village sweeping away houses, people and trees. Over three thousand individuals were killed, many of them children who were home from school on holiday. The cause was an offshore earthquake that generated three waves all striking the New Guinea coast within a twenty minute period. Where the waves came ashore, absolutely everything was carried away leaving a twenty mile stretch of beach completely barren.

Volcano Limpet, *Fissurella volcano* resembles a tiny volcano with pink stripes radiating down its sides from the hole in the top. Common.

Every so often another destructive wave, called a rogue wave hits. It appears unexpectedly and is responsible for capsizing boats and washing fishermen off breakwaters normally considered safe. An especially large rogue wave almost sank the Queen Mary in 1942 when she served as a troop ship. Hit broadside by a wave that caused her to list until her upper decks were awash, had she not slowly righted herself, a horrible accident would have occurred.

Another rogue wave hit an Italian ocean liner off New York, smashing windows eighty feet above the water line. And in July of 1992 at Daytona Beach, Florida, a wall of water eighteen feet high rose out of a calm sea crashing onto the sand, smashing hundreds of vehicles on the beach and causing seventy-five injuries. It was later determined this rogue wave was caused by an underwater landslide.

While rogue waves are rare, they do occur and are thought to be created by extreme coincidence of a variety of conditions. Two waves with exactly the same frequency converge and create a wave twice as high as normal. A sport fishing boat off Baja California, swamped and sunk by a twenty foot wave killing ten people was probably hit by this type of wave.

In life when we are confronted with a series of difficulties at the same time, it is like a rogue wave, sometimes too high to ride out. The tsunamis and rogue waves of living are no more predictable than ocean waves and, therefore, hit with surprise and shock. My rogue wave was the diagnosis of cancer. I was stunned, incapable of comprehending anything more than that I might die. I survived this wave, but I floundered around for over a year during my recovery.

I know people are hit with rogue waves of a life-threatening disease every day and some survive, while others are lost. My rogue wave was survivable. I was tossed in a sea of doctors and tests and chemical medications. But I was fortunate as life saving floats in the guise of family, friends and curing med- icine appeared at times I felt like giving up and sinking. In time I came out of the wave, bedraggled, but alive and softened by the experience.

Pacific Littleneck Clam, *Protothaca staminea*, a hard-shelled clam.

39

I sometimes recall a time when I was new to the beach and tried to bodysurf an ocean wave too big for me to handle. I was pulled down into it, churned around and tossed upon the sand like a rag. With a nose full of sea water, skinned knees and scraped elbows, I realized I'd tried to do something I wasn't ready for and counted myself lucky to survive. But it was a frightening experience I never want to repeat, just as I would also prefer not to repeat the experience of having cancer.

In the same year I was fighting cancer, a different kind of rogue wave hit me on top of the cancer wave. A natural history museum I had devoted over six years of my time to help establish, failed, leaving debts and creditors to deal with. Even though I was an unpaid volunteer, I had worked all day five days a week to establish and help run the museum. We gained membership and funds to hire a credentialed director, moved to a large building, and opened with an animated dinosaur exhibit absolutely guaranteed to bring in the crowds. Alas, our location was in a new area difficult to find, and while we had more buses of school children visit than any other museum in Orange County that year, it was not enough to pay our rent and overhead and keep the museum afloat.

During this difficult time, I was still on chemotherapy, dragging myself to board meetings, disguising my thinning hair falling out in handfuls and trying not to look sick. My dream and that of a whole group, who had been working even longer than I, dissolved into foam and mist. The one thing other than my family, I had put my heart and soul into was swept away. While this rogue wave did not threaten my life, it held me under water at a time I needed a breath of air.

In spite of the devastation I felt from this wave of change, I know I also gained in experience, insight and understanding of others who have lost livelihoods and dreams. I learned that as waves of change hit, how we are affected depends upon where we are standing at the time, on the beach or in deep water, in a secure place in our lives, or barely getting by. As we ride out the wave, we may be badly injured or only tumbled a little. Those who survive a rogue wave, learn it becomes an important part of life and growth.

Sometimes swimmers get caught in rip tides of waves and unless they know to swim sideways from the wave instead of against it, they can be carried away and lost. Perhaps if I think of the museum experience as a rip tide that took me out to sea until I learned how to swim sideways to deal with it, it will be easier to live with.

I am not so naive as to think that I will never again in my lifetime be hit by a rogue wave, carried away on a rip tide, or struck by a tsunami. What I do know from my time spent on the beach observing, experiencing, sensing, is that until another wave of change hits, I will go evenly along, realizing most waves are positive changes, some more challenging than others, but all with value.

As I walk the bluff top on this mild morning and observe rolling waves, splashing at the base of the cliff fifty feet below me, it is hard to imagine an enormous wall of water reaching the high area where I stand and seem so safe. I can only hope the tsunamis and rare rogue waves, whether water born or life experiences, will not hit my personal shore. May they stay away, out to sea or in the background venting their power without pulling me under so deep I can never again reach the surface and regain my joy of life.

Inner sides of shed crab shells.

40

Wavy Top Shell, *Astraea undosa,* also called Wavy Turban. The operculum or trapdoor-like closing for the shell's aperture or opening is brown to match the shell's exterior and white on the opposite side. The snail is protected when the operculum is closed.

Waves washed this styrofoam with barnacles and mussels onto the beach. California Mussel, *Mytilus californianus*, attaches to rocks and pilings, color bluish - black. Pink Barnacles, *Balanus tintinnabulum*, are pinkish red with white vertical stripes. They attach to anything solid in the water, including other shells and man - made debris like this piece of styrofoam. The Pink Barnacles at the bottom left have another smaller, brown type attached to them.

Boat

a struggle with the sea

"In nature there are neither rewards or punishments -- There are consequences."

Robert G. Ingersoll

Waves with six foot faces boil onto the sand with thunderous roars. Hard breaking surf rushes up the sloping beach, spends its fury and drains back down the incline to collide with the next wave slamming shoreward. This morning the aftermath of a Pacific storm rules the sea and leaves reminders on land of its ruthless power.

At Pelican Point a small sailboat tipped on its side scrapes across sharp stone ledges as each new wave pushes the already battered craft further onto shore. The heavy keel designed to keep the boat upright in deep water drags uselessly on uneven ground. Unable to help, I watch wave after wave pound the boat, grinding it heavily over sand and jagged rocks. Its mortal wound, a gaping hole in the blue fiber glass hull, bleeds splinters of interior fittings. The mast, separated from the boat, lies dismantled and bent at the base of the bluff. Red trim around the blue gunwale still proudly displays its name, My Tie.

Moving closer, I notice a dead semi-disemboweled fish hanging from one of the metal fittings. The fish, now food for circling sea gulls, and probably another victim of the storm, may have been placed there by an earlier beach walker. Like the fish, the boat with its torn hull also spills its vital organs to the sea as chunks of styrofoam leak onto the sand and wash away in the surf.

I watch as each new wave vents its fury upon the "My Tie." It becomes painful listening to the hollow grinding sounds of the hull twisting and grating on the rocks. The continuous beating of the already battered and broken craft is so violent I can no longer stand to watch. So I hurry away to distance myself from the death sounds of the dying boat.

Beach debris

As I continue my beachwalk, the boat's battle with the sea stays with me. I think of a good friend of mine who helped her sister endure the final days of a losing fight against lung cancer. How difficult it must have been to watch the pounding and battering of a loved one as death neared. While I am saddened by the My Tie's struggle, my friend must have felt her sister's pain with an intensity that I can't even imagine. How did she nurse her sister and keep from being dragged under with her own grief and emotional hurt? Did she, too, sometimes have to walk away to distance herself from the battle with the disease in order to stay afloat? Perhaps later and after some healing, a time will come when we can talk honestly about her experience.

Returning from my walk, I again pick my way across the rugged rocky shelf at Pelican Point where the sad little My Tie fights against the sea. On my approach gulls pecking at the disemboweled fish fly up with a clatter of wings and circle above. The fish, hanging in shreds, falls from its makeshift hook and disappears into the surf. It has a purpose there, even in death, as numerous sea creatures will quickly ingest its remains. Continuous cycles of life and death in the wild leave no waste, but not so with the poor ruined My Tie. As it dies, it not only loses its graceful beauty and usefulness, but it scars the beach with its broken body and creates hazards from its fittings and hardware wrenched free by the waves.

My Tie

Weathered small fragments of sea-scoured debris from man made objects.

The next morning as I take my beachwalk and arrive at Pelican Point, expecting scattered wreckage from massive damage to the beached boat, I am surprised to see all remains of the My Tie are gone, including the broken mast and interior seat boards, which had been stacked in a neat pile on shore. The My Tie has been rescued from its grueling ordeal. I search for signs of its struggle I so painfully identified with the day before. But all that is left to remind me of yesterday's duel with the sea is a series of blue paint streaks ground onto the rocks near shore.

A wood fragment with rusted nails and encrusted with the bottom halves of California Oysters, *Ostrea lurida*. Irregular in shape, these oyster shells conform to the outlines of the object on which they grow.

46

Whales
hope for mankind

"One touch of nature makes the whole world kin."

William Shakespeare

Covered with sweat, my windbreaker plastered to my back from fine mist in the pale morning, my walk nearly finished, I climb the drainage channel to head for home, a warm shower and some breakfast. At the top of the bluff I pause and turn back for one last look at the sandy shoreline and seemingly infinite sea spread before me. There, in the middle of my living seascape, an enormous dark shape explodes from the gray water amid a cloak of foam and spray. Twisting in mid air, the whale throws sheets of water skyward as it crashes back into the white-capped waves. I stand almost paralyzed with amazement and awe, watching, as another gigantic black shape rises from the depths, spirals in the air and splashes down into waves and foam. "Whales, breaching," I whisper aloud, as I stand, afraid to blink, for fear I will miss an instant of this incredible sight.

This was my first breathtaking whale watching experience at Crystal Cove. Other times, I had witnessed whales spouting, spewing columns of moist, hot breath into the air as they surfaced to breathe. I had marveled at the sight of their two-lobed, black, tail flukes flipping gracefully above the water's surface in preparation for a deep dive. But had it not been my habit to pause on the bluff top at the end of my walk for one final appreciative look at the primal beauty of this beach, I would have missed this rare moment of spectacular behavior.

While it is Gray whales I commonly see migrating along the California coast from their northern feeding grounds in Alaska to birthing lagoons in Baja, Mexico - a 12,000 mile journey - Humpback whales occasionally also appear in these waters. One day as I walked up the concrete steps from a small beach fronting Cameo Shores where I live, an acquaintance sun bathing on the sand below, called out to me. "Whales!" she shouted, her voice barely audible above the sound of crashing surf. I turned in time to see a huge black fin slap down next to a black back above the waves. I knew from the distinctive long pectoral that these were

Humpbacks and not Grays. A mother and her newborn calf were performing a slow whale ballet just beyond the breaking surf. At least one other adult whale, perhaps two were with them. Often several large dark shapes appeared at the same time, as I watched a huge fin rise from the water, point skyward and lazily flop back into the sea. Sometimes the small pointed head of the calf popped straight up for a few seconds before sinking out of sight. Puffs of hot breath spouted upward, leaving spumes of white vapor hanging briefly in the air as a token of the creatures below. The heavy, whoosh sound of expelled breath was so loud, it sang above the surf and sent a shiver of excitement down my back as it pulled me spiritually towards the whales.

Humpback Whale, *Megapetra novaengliae*, in breaching behavior. It is thought whales throw themselves out of the water in order to dislodge barnacles.

48

I have had special feelings towards Humpbacks ever since a trip to Hawaii where I heard one "singing." Treading water with my head just below the surface, I listened to a series of haunting, melodious notes, some long and drawn out, others short like bird chirps. I was overwhelmed with emotion to hear for myself, a whale in the wild, communicating with its kind. I will never forget the sound as it lingers in my ears and fills me with tenderness for these gigantic creatures.

I have never seen a Blue Whale, which is not only the largest whale, but also the largest animal ever to have inhabited the earth. Bigger than a Boeing 747 and weighing six times more, its heart alone is the size of a Volkswagen car. In July of 1980, a 52-foot long baby Blue Whale carcass weighing 60 tons drifted into Los Angeles Harbor. Had it lived to adulthood, it could have reached 100 feet in length and weighed 150 tons. There have been sightings of Blue Whales north of here and someday if I'm really lucky maybe I'll have the thrill of seeing one.

Meanwhile, I watch for signs of Gray Whales on their annual migration along this southern California coast. These are the spouts I witness on those special mornings when whales are close to shore. If I happened to have my binoculars, I have sometimes seen tiny flukes surface near a mother, as I focused on the misty spume of whale breath. It always gives me a thrill to spot a whale and be reminded they are still here and have recovered from near extinction after years of heavy whaling.

A Gray Whale, *Eschrichtiys glaucus,* spyhopping - scanning the horizon.

Humpbacks and Gray Whales are generally docile and not a threat to people, but there are occasional incidences of aggressive behavior. In 1981, a body surfer spotted a pod of Gray Whales off Laguna Beach, just south of Crystal Cove. After swimming toward them, a 30-foot whale pushed him head over heels out of the water. He suffered a bruised kidney, internal bleeding and various aches and pains. It was assumed the whale was being protective because of the number of young in the pod.

That same year another surfer at Zuma Beach to the north was hit by a single twitch of a 6-foot wide whale tail that lifted him upward about 8 feet and threw him outward another 10. While neither surfer in the two incidents was seriously injured, both experienced an unexpected and potentially life threatening trauma, reminding us that whales need space and when we intrude upon their environment, we are no match for these gigantic sea-going mammals.

Whales were on earth long before man and after their beginnings in ancient seas, spent time on land. Their ancestors were around 55 million years ago, when as land animals they returned to the water. Fossil whales found inland from Crystal Cove in Orange County have been dated as old as 14 million years. Evidence of human life in Orange County is closer to only 14 thousand.

The whales have more experience of generations than we do. As we study and get to know them better, perhaps their fight for survival over the millenia will provide lessons for our survival and that of the planet.

Gray Whale tail flukes appear above water in preparation for a deep dive.

Gray Whales are baleen whales and mature to 35 - 50 feet in length and 20 - 40 tons. This is the whale that migrates from the Bering Sea along the California coast to calve in the warm lagoons of Baja, Mexico.

On my daily walks during the winter whale season, my eyes are always busy scanning the horizon for whale spouts. When I see one, it is my gift for the morning, but the best sightings occur when least expected. One day after I was drenched with rain and hurrying home from my beachwalk, the sky began to clear and a rainbow appeared out over the ocean. As I stood for a last look in my usual spot on the bluff top, watching spectrum colors brighten in the sun with red melting into orange, yellow and finally indigo, two whales spouted under the rainbow's arc, leaving their white spumes of breath as an additional reminder to me of hope for the whales, hope for mankind and hope for the world we share.

Scents
evoking memories

"*Pleasure is the flower that fades; remembrance is the lasting perfume.*"

S. Boufflers

The sand-paved horse trail I follow across the bluff top is lined with rows of Telegraph Weeds towering above my head like cornstalks in a country cornfield. Their dry leaves, brown and dusty, rattle as a tender ocean breeze from the beach below lifts itself up over the edge of the bluffs and travels lightly inland. Crinkled leaves on dry twigs rustle as I brush against them and a noisy fly buzzes around a clump of dried Encelia blooms. Only a few weeks ago they were still in full flower, their leaves a fuzzy, sage green, their small multi-rayed flowers bright yellow.

I inhale deeply to capture the scent of fall in the air. The smell is warm and dusty, like aromatic herbs and dry grasses. It is the smell of the end of summer when green spring plants have turned brown and brittle, sun-baked to a crackly crispness. It is a good smell, like hay in a haymow or crumpled fall leaves. It is a potent smell that overpowers the odor of the sea below. It is a smell that triggers a childhood memory of sitting outside on the wooden stoop of our farm house in rural Minnesota, breathing in the fragrance of cut grass and listening to the drone of one pesky fly buzzing nearby. I can still feel warm sun on my back and remember how I felt at that moment. Encased in childhood innocence, free of responsibility, a world of possibilities ahead with infinite time to realize them, I was surrounded by a pure and simple tranquillity; its picture imprinted so strongly upon my inner self, it has remained

Seaweed is actually an algae because it does not have roots, stems and leaves even though it may have similar-looking structures. The four major groups of algae are named for their colors, blue-green, green, red and brown. This piece of brown algae has a colony of stalked barnacles growing on it.

part of me to this day. The earthy, dry, grassy smell of this morning projects this memory picture upon my inner screen as if I had punched an "ON" switch.

As I make my way down the gravel wash to water and beach below, crisp ocean air full of dampness and salt fills my nostrils. I recognize the scent of the sea coming from a multitude of individual odors melding into one characteristic ocean smell. Sometimes I think of it as fishy, but strangely enough, it is not fish so much as seaweed and algae that make up what we generally think of as a fishy smell. On some days, decaying piles of kelp reeking of ammonia blot out the usual ocean essence with a sharp, acrid, nose-bending stench, second only to the stink of rotting piles of Blue Mussels decaying after storm waves dislodged them from their rocky anchorages.

But generally the smell of the beach is not one of decay, but instead a medley of odors emanating from living things. It is the tangy tobacco-like scent of ice plant growing on sandstone cliffs. It is the piquant and spicy smell of crushed sage and wild herbs that hangs in the air and mingles with whiffs of wet earth and rock and weathering hunks of driftwood. It is the soft mustiness that drifts out of washes cut deeper into the bluff with each rain.

Looking back , it is the same damp earth smell that hung in the air around springs and boggy spots where I grew up in the Midwest. Behind my house was an empty lot connected to a wild natural creek that ran all summer long. With the leisure and focus of children at play, I searched for pollywogs in the early spring and stalked noisy green-spotted, warty frogs to catch in my hand and then let go. I worried their warts might really be catching as I had been told so often. But always the damp earth, green cattail scent was there. I smell that same odor here in the wash draining the coastal terrace above the beach. But instead of cattails, wild cane thrives on the stream's edges and at the end of the growing season it clogs the channel and forces drainage water to fan out on to the sand as it makes its way to the sea.

This morning I sense a faint and pleasant charcoal odor of burned driftwood, but further on a small plume of acrid smoke still rising from last night's beach bonfire assaults my nostrils. I feel suffocated and I want to get away from it as quickly as possible. I am especially sensitive to smoke so that even a small whiff of a burning cigarette or cigar taints the fresh beach air with a disagree-ableness that intrudes upon the distinct redolence of the sea.

I often sense a faint odor of tar when I'm at the beach and sometimes even after I arrive home with small globs of the sticky stuff glued to my shoes. While I think of tar as a man made substance because of its use on roofs and roads, it is really a natural occurrence issuing from underground oil deposits that leak out into the ocean. At times the delicate tide pools harboring small sea life actually reek of tar from chunks of it washed shoreward and caught in crevices between rocks.

While I don't appreciate stepping on beach tar and carrying it home on my shoes, I must remember it was once an especially useful substance for early native inhabitants of this shore. They used tar as a kind of multipurpose glue, plugging holes in large abalone shells with sticky globs to create bowls and scoops. And in the Los Angeles area 60 miles to the north there is a large surface deposit of tar known as the La Brea tar pits. A museum there chronicles the Pleistocene era of 50 to 100 thousand years ago when mammoths, saber toothed tigers and dire wolves roamed the land. Their remains are preserved in the tar pits, where they came to drink surface water and were trapped to die a cruel death in the sticky deposits below the surface. Today, oil spills from tankers create a similar hazard for shorebirds and small intertidal sea life.

But tar isn't the only offender. With major development taking place in the hills across the highway I am sometimes assaulted with the smell of diesel exhaust if the wind is from the land. It makes me gag and soils my beachwalk. It also brings back another childhood memory of long bus rides I took each summer from southern Wisconsin to northern Minnesota. At each bus stop, the stink of diesel fumes belched from the back of the bus in a gray cloud, polluting the air and making me feel sick to my stomach. The nauseating smell made me hate the bus ride even though I liked going to spend the summer with my sisters and brothers, whom I did not live with during the winter.

I was four years old when my mother died leaving six month old twins and seven older children. My Great Aunt Elsie, after attending the funeral, took me home with her on a temporary basis until my dad could get things under control. As it turned out, Aunt Elsie kept me and raised me in Wisconsin during the school year and sent me back to the farm on a lake in Minnesota each summer to be with my family. She was in her sixties when she took responsibility for me, a four year old, and she always said it kept her young. It was not a bad arrangement for me either, since I had the advantages of being an only child during the school year and with my eight siblings during the summer months.

It was with these siblings during summer vacations that I developed much of my love for nature. My older brothers shared hidden birds' nests, pointed out sweet smelling wild roses that grew along field fences, and led me through birch thickets to stands of wild raspberry bushes. Our farm bordered a lake where we swam, fished and played. That's where I learned that small leeches, we called blood suckers, lurked in the bulrushes and snapping turtles rested on floating logs. Both were to be avoided. The blood suckers often won and had to be pulled from between our toes or the backs of our knees. Perhaps they helped me feel comfortable swimming in ocean water, since I've never come upon anything as disgusting as those lake leeches.

While the Minnesota lake had a water and plant and fish smell, it was completely different from the ocean water and seaweed smell of the beach. I can identify either in a second. I read the words, "smell of the sea," many times in books and I always feel as if I know exactly what it is. It is plants and water and rock and decay and tar and mustiness and so many other things, a long recipe slightly different for each day and place. But there is another quality, elusive and tantalizing that I can't define. Sometimes I think I smell it when I'm away from it, but it's real essence eludes me and stays just out of reach.

Each of us has certain nostalgic scents that conjure up past images. As we are the sum of our experiences, scent memories make powerful contributions to life's meaning. A pleasure picture that flashes into my mind, triggered by a past smell adds to my happiness. The scent inspired pictures that dredge up bad memories, I try to tape over with a new and better version. For many years, I hated the smell of apple juice because it brought back the unpleasantness of drinking an anti-nausea drug in apple juice when I was going through chemotherapy for cancer. Little by little I have replaced the dreaded apple smell image with the idea of a crisp, fresh apple as a healthy food, one that is good for my body. I still don't relish apple juice, but I have learned to drink it without bad memories.

Smells that recall pleasurable events or those I want to remember because they were special in some way, I easily retain. I don't want my scent memories to fade away and escape my perception. I want them to seep into my soul and give me comfort.

Recently as I was spraying on perfume in my four year old granddaughter's presence, she wanted some, too. As I gave her a small sample, she sniffed and said, "Oh, yes, Gramma, you always smell like that." I hope that someday, perhaps when I'm gone, a brief whiff of my perfume will trigger a scent memory for her and good thoughts of her grandmother will pop to the surface.

Sun Cup, *Oenothera bistorta*, an annual found in sandy or dry disturbed places. Flowers have dark spots near their centers and begin flowering in January.

54

Leaving the beach today with its smell of the sea etched so deeply upon my senses and crossing the dry aromatic fields on my way home, I breathe deeply to program their scents into my permanent memory bank. There they will remain stored and safe, ready to be called up at some future time to trigger the happy memories they represent.

Cowry shells are found in tropical seas. The Chestnut Cowry, *Cypraea spadica,* is egg-shaped, polished and the only true cowry that gets as far north as southern California.

Coffee Bean, *Trivia Californiana,* was the first unusual shell to pique my curiosity when I moved to the beach. My daughter found the first one and later every one I came upon seemed like a treasure. The shell is the size of a coffee bean, but not the color. I saw the bright scarlet animal inside only once while snorkeling. It was clinging to a tall strand of kelp.

-Apple Seed, *Erato vitellina,* lives in seaweeds. It is about 1/2 inch long and reddish brown.

One day I found this broken terra cotta bottle. It was the same color as a small
scallop shell and some wind blown dry leaves smelling of fall.

56

Death

a natural process

"I am not afraid of storms for I am learning how to sail my ship."
Louisa May Alcott

The dried, shriveled carcass of a baby Sea Lion lies splayed upon the sand in a bed of seaweed. Orange kelp fronds twist around the small body. One shoulder juts out in a hump, skin stretched tightly around the emaciated form. Just another death on the beach, I tell myself, so I won't feel so sad about this little creature, who had such a short chance at life. Is it any different, I think, than the nearby Red Crab lying upside down, its breast hollowed out by a scavenging black crow, or the gull with a broken wing, lurking far up on the sand in an effort to stay away from the water's edge, where it has no place to hide. As I approach, the gull waddles further away from me, its dragging wing leaving a furrow in the sand, and I can only be reminded that it, too, will soon succumb to the perils of its environment. Even an empty clam shell, which ordinarily would please me with its symmetrical beauty and delicate off white color, today, registers, instead, as another death on the beach.

These beach deaths bring my thoughts to other deaths that are close to me; a nephew recently passed away from cancer. I write the words, "passed away," and flinch at their euphemistic use. Would I ever say the baby sea lion "passed away;" the clam "passed away?" Or is it only people who "pass away" because it is so hard to say "died?" Why must I deny that living flesh dies and decays? What happens to the soul is another matter. Whether one's soul lives on or passes to another place or dimension depends upon individual beliefs.

Kellet's Whelk, *Kelletia Kelleti*. A rugged, heavy shell as large as 6 inches. One of the largest gastropods on the West Coast.

But how is it with animals? Does a starving or sick Sea Lion know its death is approaching, or is it only humans who are able to think about the future? The husband of one of my good friends has been diagnosed with stage IV lung cancer. It is inoperable and no reliable chemotherapy is available, although they will try different kinds.

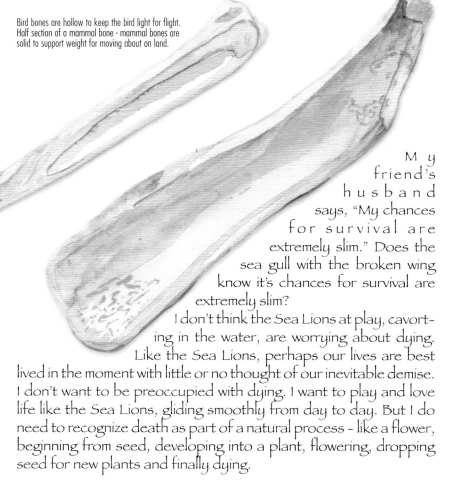

Bird bones are hollow to keep the bird light for flight. Half section of a mammal bone - mammal bones are solid to support weight for moving about on land.

My friend's husband says, "My chances for survival are extremely slim." Does the sea gull with the broken wing know it's chances for survival are extremely slim?

I don't think the Sea Lions at play, cavorting in the water, are worrying about dying. Like the Sea Lions, perhaps our lives are best lived in the moment with little or no thought of our inevitable demise. I don't want to be preoccupied with dying. I want to play and love life like the Sea Lions, gliding smoothly from day to day. But I do need to recognize death as part of a natural process - like a flower, beginning from seed, developing into a plant, flowering, dropping seed for new plants and finally dying.

58

The bright light celebrating birth and the continuation of life blinds me to the inevitability of death, which lurks in the shadows, hides in corners and crevices staying unknown, out of reach, until the day it leaps out and must be faced.

My friend's husband is putting his affairs in order and making arrangements for his body after death. I think about the difficulty of planning for my own demise. I, and most people, I think, are strangely unprepared for an event which will definitely occur. Until we are forced to face it, we ignore it and act as if it won't happen to us.

My own bout with cancer took me from playing mindlessly with eternal life to the beginning of some understanding of my mortality. After the diagnosis and realization I might die, one of my thoughts was the need to clean out drawers and boxes of saved items no one else would want. How petty, but even as I was faced with my death, I still couldn't really comprehend or accept it. So I transferred my fear to practical measures, activities I could do while waiting.

I was clinging to life and all those little things we do with our time when we think tomorrow will come as usual. But now as years pass separating me from the cancer experience, I can feel myself drifting back to living as if I will be around forever. As each day of good heath prevails, it gets harder and harder to acknowledge my inevitable "passing away."

I grieve a little for each dead creature I come upon on my daily walks. The sea gull with the broken wing hurts me even more because I know its fate and I am a witness to the futile battle it is waging to live. Earlier this week I came upon a Harbor Seal stretched out on a warm patch of sand. With sad dark eyes, it was still breathing, but too sick to move. Long lashes ringed its limpid eyes that half opened as I paused to gaze at the suffering creature. It could never last the twenty-four hour waiting period required by Friends of the Sea Lion rescue group. It was too late. I chased away two jet black crows that were heckling it, but they would soon be back pecking at those beautiful eyes.

It would be nice never to be reminded of sad or troubling things on my beachwalk. But the beach is in many ways, a microcosm of the world in which I live, and that's a large part of what makes it so appealing to me. If the beach were all happiness and beauty every day, it could not sustain my interest and devotion over the years. It would have little relationship to my life. Just as I must dig in the sand to uncover beach treasures, I need my beachwalk to help me dig beneath the surface of everyday events in order to find their buried meanings.

Today, my beachwalk makes me think about death, death as a part of life, and while I feel sadness, I also feel a new wholeness and kinship with other living creatures. While our life spans are very different in the wide range of species inhabiting the earth, our bodies still share a common destiny. The life cycle we share validates our connection more than our DNA differences estrange us.

My concern today is with the death of the body, not of the soul, and whether creatures other than humans have souls, I do not know. With or without a soul, they are deserving of my respect. I stop to cover the pitiful body of the baby Sea Lion. I scoop up sand with a piece of flat driftwood and heap it on top of the small form leaving a sandy mound on the beach. I drop the driftwood scoop and head for the beach gate and back to the world where friends and family need my attention and where I will do what I can to ease the pain of death when it confronts me.

I cannot resist picking up feathers from the beach sands. I'm always curious about how each one was shed.

Totems
beachwalk reminders

"The true wonder of the world is available everywhere, in the minutest parts of our bodies, in the vast expanses of the cosmos, and in the interconnectedness of these and all things."

Michael Stark

The day begins with a thin shelf of gray clouds hanging over a noisy metallic sea. To the south, scattered patches of darker sky cast deep purple shadows onto the water below. A stiff breeze from the northwest flattens my light windbreaker against my back and ruffles my hair. I watch a red and white styrofoam lobster float bounce up and down against the rocks at Pelican Point as the incoming tide struggles to free it from the braided nylon rope and wire trap wedged between two large boulders. Long strands of brown kelp half buried in the sand twist around the yellow rope, anchoring it even more securely among the rocks. I wonder if I can get close enough to cut its bindings and carry the red and white cylinder home with me as a prized addition to the lobster floats I've collected over the years.

For as long as I've been coming to this beach, every stray float I've found cast upon the sand has ended up in my yard. "Why?" I ask myself. "What is there about finding something on the beach that compels me to carry it home?" I certainly have no good use for a multitude of stray lobster buoys. Their bright paint box colors of purple, yellow, orange, red and green attract me. But surely their appeal is more than just color. Many were so difficult to separate from the long lines securing them to their wire traps that I now carry a small jackknife in my beachwalk pack. I use it primarily to rescue birds caught in loops of fishing line, but it also comes in handy to sever the thick nylon rope attached to a beached lobster float. It takes firm pressure and a long time to saw through each sturdy strand of braided nylon and I usually end up with blisters from my effort. Sometimes I'm lucky and can untie the knots, and sometimes I have to give

up and leave the float in its bed of sand and seaweed. I realize the float caught in the rocks today is one of those teasers, so I leave it to continue its dance with the surf.

The floats I have carried home, form a symbolic binding strand that stretches from land to sea and back again. They are objects manufactured for use in the water, but rejected by the sea and thrown back onto the land. As I collect them, one by one, they are my connectors to the beach and ocean as well as reminders of the joy I derive from my daily beachwalks.

In a way, they are much like sea shells, so appealing on the beach, but when I get them home, it's often hard to find a place for them. As my eyes feast on their bright painted hues standing out against the tan sand, each vibrantly colored buoy becomes a bit of pop art displayed in an outdoor gallery. They call out, begging to be acquired just as a pink shell on the tide-washed sand must be picked up and examined.

The first ones I brought home, I tried hanging on the inside of a fence at the side of our yard. I was inspired by scenes of picturesque fishing villages. I could see the floats from my kitchen window and while I had expected them to be interesting and pleasant, they looked really junky. My husband, ever tolerant of my idiosyncrasies, never said a word and even helped hang them for me. When we moved to a different house, five blocks away, the floats moved with us. That's when they settled in my secret garden and became beach totems. More than a symbol now, they are tangible objects representing my kinship and almost mystical relationship with the ocean beach.

Small painted wooden fishing floats.

Over two hundred floats strung vertically on rebar pounded into the ground under a bushy tree, stand in a group like skinny people. Each "person" consists of four or five floats and stands about fifty inches tall. Hidden from the house, small portions of the grouping can be glimpsed from the street below. Just enough of them shows through the leafy branches that every now and then I get a contribution from a neighbor who throws a float over my fence or leaves one on my doorstep knowing it will have a home in the secret garden. It makes me feel good that I'm not alone in my addiction of picking up beached lobster buoys and that others find them irresistible as well.

My multicolor beach totems in the leaf covered garden clearing remind me of Hopi Kachinas in dance formation. I can almost picture them stomping in rhythmic unison to the musical pound of waves breaking on shore. At other times, I think of the carved and painted eagles and whales on totem poles of the Haida people in the Northwest. My totems, however, have no carved images of birds or animals. Their only engraving is a set of numbers burned into the plastic foam.

For native tribes and clans, totems serve as reminders of ancestry and lineage. My simple, brightly colored totems, instead, serve as reminders of my beachwalk, my refuge, my place

of contemplation and serenity. Installed as they are in my secret garden, they bring the inner peace of the beach to my home, keeping the spirit of my beachwalk with me as I enjoy my garden.

There will come a time when I will move from the house where I now live. I already know the lobster float totems will not move with me a second time. When I leave this house I will be finished with my totems and will no longer have a need for their presence in my life. I will be simplifying, letting go, and focusing on a new phase of living. The time for collecting will have passed and other things will be important in its place. As with most collections, the fun is in the hunt and the wise collector knows when to give up the collection.

But today I am still enjoying the hunt. Perhaps, on my next beachwalk, the red-and-white float that eludes me this morning will be freed from its ropes and seaweed, ready to join the many others that give me pleasure in my garden.

A sampling of fishing lures and bobber.

Examples of different colors and types of braiding used in plastic nautical ropes. These were all beach finds.

Treasures
recognizing rewards

"There is no thrill like discovery."
unknown

ennies green with oxidation from salt water, a half dollar blackened with age, a few nickels and a dime rest in my hand, where I hold them tightly as I search the rocky crevices for more treasure. I call this northwest side of Pelican Point "the treasure cracks," because things wash up here and get wedged in shallow channels where the massive rock point has splintered and pulled apart. Along with coins, the cracks harbor oxidized nuts and bolts, small metal fragments, part of a lead bullet and some brass screws turned verdigris green, just like the brass lion heads on my front gate. In trying to preserve their brass finish, I spent many hours polishing away the green oxidation until I finally decided to let the sea air win. As I scan the treasure cracks, I spot a celluloid guitar pick caught between two slivers of rock. It seems an unlikely object for a beach find, so immediately my mind begins to conjure up a fantasy story to explain its presence. Two lovers, and a romantic sunset serenade come to mind. Although I am well aware the real journey of the guitar pick to the treasure cracks would probably far surpass my fictional account.

Most of the year the treasure cracks are covered with sand. Only during a short time in the winter when storm waves scour the beach exposing its underlying rock foundation do they share their hidden secrets. But summer, too, can sometimes be rewarding as high tides leave their offerings on top of the sand. I especially remember one morning on an early beach jog, when I came upon a wallet washed up at the treasure cracks. It was wet and heavy with sand packed in every pocket along with some dollar bills. But as I began counting ones, a few tens, some twenties it added up to a total of $450. With a sense of shock I continued to brush away excess sand until I uncovered a Texas drivers license and some very wet family pictures. Thinking it probably belonged

to someone on vacation, I was concerned his holiday might be ruined by the wallet's loss. But at least I had an address where I could send it, so ultimately he would get it back.

When I returned home from my run, I searched the billfold carefully and took out the pictures and documents so they wouldn't dry stuck together. Among the items, I found a list of phone numbers, one of which was labeled, "Mom and Dad," with the area code of Laguna Beach just five miles away. When I called the number, the owner of the wallet answered the phone. A young man visiting from Texas, he told me the day before he had been with friends scuba diving several miles up coast from Pelican Point. When he discovered his wallet was missing from the back pocket of his swim trunks, he thought it would be on the sea bottom below their boat.

Guitar pick

They continued diving to search for it through a good part of the evening using rented lights. Finally they conceded it was gone for good. Never could they have imagined it would turn up twelve hours later and two miles away at my treasure cracks.

The wallet's treasure for me wasn't its dollar value, but instead the thrill of my handing it to someone who was so surprised and grateful to get it back. I know I felt as excited about returning it to the young man, as he did on receiving it. I was left with an inner glow, that intrinsic reward of feeling good knowing I had been able to help a complete stranger. Another time I found a watch, but after leaving notices taped to the beach stairway for several weeks, I never received a call. So the watch ended up on my daughter's wrist and she still wears it years later.

Beaches don't always give up their treasure so easily and sometimes hide it for years, yielding it unexpectedly only after a storm or shift in sand deposition. In 1981, on Goleta Beach near Santa Barbara north of Crystal Cove, five ancient cannons from the 1700's were uncovered by a Pacific storm. Encrusted with tar and embedded with pebbles, the cannons looked more like pieces of old sewer pipe than historical treasures. The discoverer of the artifacts had a hard time getting an authority to look at them until he finally contacted the University of California at Santa Barbara. A year later the cannons still had not been absolutely identified, even after X-ray examination confirmed enough characteristics to suspect the guns might be relics from one of Sir Francis Drake's voyages in the 16th century. Drake is known to have hauled out the Golden Hind for repairs near Santa Barbara and the ancient ship's logs confirm that some cannons were left behind.

At Pelican Point, I kick at a rusty mass of old metal covered with bits of shell and pebbles cemented together with tar and I wonder if it is something old and important. I think if cannons from Sir Francis Drake's Golden Hind can emerge from beach sands after hundreds of years, who knows what other treasures are still waiting for discovery. But since I can't identify any part of the clump of fused metal at my feet, I leave it and walk on.

Another secret of the beach sands that surfaced after the heavy storms of 1981 was unearthed by two scuba divers from three feet of water at Sunset Beach to the north. A clump of World War II relics including mortar rounds, launchers, projectiles, anti-aircraft ammunition and other dangerous items was found grouped together in a cement-like substance. Before calling the Navy, the two divers hammered heavily on the block to separate the items, but fortunately for them, without success.

As it turned out, much of the ammunition was live. No one, including the Navy, had any idea where these blocks of memorabilia came from.

Which reminds me, there is always a possibility that beach treasure can be dangerous, since potentially harmful items are often dumped in the ocean with the idea that the sea will swallow them forever. But the ocean is capricious and releases long lost deposits at unexpected moments. So it is with our personal lives. I have dumped disturbing images and ideas into my personal "get rid of" file and I think they are gone, only to have them surface when I least expect it. They lie covered, out of sight and mind, most of the time, but lurking hidden and waiting for the storm of change that will uncover them. I push them back into my subconscious, bury them in my sandy recesses, still knowing they will intrude into my thoughts at some unpredictable time. I would like to dig up my buried images and remove them forever, like historical beach relics uncovered and taken away, but I must wait for the right storms of life, the cleansing tumult that leaves a clean palette.

The handful of coins, rusty nails and guitar pick I gathered today at the treasure cracks can hardly qualify as real treasure, but the finding of it stimulates the treasure idea which is often more exciting and real than treasure itself. It is the idea of discovery that keeps treasure seekers on their quests. From kids with metal detectors scanning the beach to sophisticated and highly financed ships and equipment, the search for treasure goes on.

I, like so many others, am a treasure hunter. I search daily and I always find treasure. It may be a pretty shell, a dolphin surfacing off shore, a rainbow, a spouting whale, a nice comment from a stranger, the feel of warm sun on my back. These are the treasures I value. While I think of the beach as my place to treasure hunt, as I leave for home, I know there is treasure everywhere and I will continue always to look for it wherever I am.

Three-winged Rock Shell, *Pterynotsus trialatus*. I treasure these beautiful shallow water shells. They occasionally appear on the beach.

Storm Birds

refuge from the rain

*"The man killed the bird, and with the bird he killed the song,
and with the song, himself."*

From a Pygmy legend

A cold, hard winter rain drenches the land and sea alike and deters me from my early morning beachwalk. As I look out my water-spotted window, I see two doves huddled in the low branches of an Acacia tree waiting out the storm. As soon as it stops raining, I know they will check the bird feeder on the windward side of my house for sunflower seeds and the grains they gobble up so quickly. I can also see a few Bushtits sheltered under the leafy branches of the same tree and I think of how often I've wondered where birds go when it rains. Now I have an answer for birds I see in my yard, but I still wonder about shorebirds. Where do sea gulls, pelicans, cormorants, grebes and all those little sandpipers go when winds howl and rain pelts down with fierce force? An Audubon Society guide once told me they go out to sea and ride the waves.

Sheets of rain continue to pound the ground and gusty winds drive across the garden pushing over deck chairs and the sun umbrella. The ocean looks steely-gray with angry, white capped waves roiling towards shore. Are there really flocks of shorebirds out there waiting for an end to the bad weather? During a lull in the storm's intensity, three pelicans and a gray gull fly past my window, and again, I wonder, where have they come from and where are they going?

Like the doves sheltering in my Acacia tree, I am holed up in my studio to wait out the inclement weather. The few times I've been on the beach in the rain, I am always impressed with the wild, primal quality of the fog-shrouded, windswept shore. Weather, a state over which we have no control, seems to have enormous control over us. With all of our acquired knowledge enabling the building of skyscrapers, exploration of space and the production of enough nuclear power to blow up our planet, we are still at the mercy of a simple rainstorm, snarling traffic, causing flooding, and altering our moods.

Birds, too, suffer from the effects of nature's power. After a storm, the beach is often littered with the debris of its victims. Bedraggled, feathered carcasses lie in contorted poses on piles of driftwood and in sandy semi-graves. Sometimes I carefully observe their broken bodies to see if I can figure out the cause of their deaths. Other times I can't bear to dwell on their sad and pitiful remains and I hurry past.

Last week my happy beach experience was brought up short by a male Surf Scoter with an injured leg prohibiting it from taking flight. I don't often see these beautiful birds on my beachwalks. About the size of a duck, their humped bright orange and white beak punctuated with a black spot, and their bright white neck patch, easily distinguish them from other black-bodied sea birds like grebes and cormorants. As I passed by, his head turned and he followed me with a wary eye. "Would I be a threat to him?" I moved away quickly to show he had nothing to fear from me, but it gave me no peace. Knowing that other animals, other birds and even other unthinking people would see him as prey and all of his attempts at survival would ultimately fail. I felt frustrated I could not help.

Sadness for the bird and what he was experiencing colored my normally joyous beach song a dismal gray, turning it into a keening dirge. I would have liked to ignore the Surf Scoter, pretend I didn't see him and his misery, but I couldn't. I knew the crows would be pecking at him as soon as he lost strength to fight back.

Two days later, the Surf Scoter lay dead in the swash line, its body nearly gone. Two bare breast bones sticking up like the curved wooden ribs of a beached and decaying miniature ship marked his short existence in the visible world.

On the beach, crows peck at the eyes of injured animals and fight over the remains of dead gulls. I think about human suffering and how courageous people approach death after enduring injury, illness and sometimes "a pecking" of raw wounds by their own species. I ask the inevitable question, "Why must there be suffering?" The only answer I know is that suffering is the opposite of joy and to know real joy and peace, I must understand the whole range of emotions.

For today, the normally blue-green ocean I see through my window has turned a muddy tan near shore, with a distinct band of dark blue-gray along the horizon. Each of the arroyos, washes and rivers emptying into the sea brings its own mud, sand and brushy deposit, coloring the clear water with rivers of brown. Every storm drain carries rain water laced with debris from our streets directly into the sea. Pesticides from lawn and garden applications, grease and oil from vehicles, toxins, chemicals and trash all end up in the ocean near shore.

Yesterday, two Black-Bellied Plovers were having a bath in the fresh water stream that drains onto the beach near the western access stairway. The spot they picked was directly beneath a sign that reads, "Danger Contaminated Water". Too bad the plovers can't read.

We all count on the cleansing action of the sea. Each high tide scouring the shore, leaving it devoid of footprints and small debris is like a broom, sweeping the beach twice a day. Rain is the mop that swabs the land. Mop water runs into the ocean, which we expect to function like a purification plant, filtering out our human waste. But we expect too much. The water at Crystal Cove remains generally good, but beaches to the north and south have been closed frequently due to unsafe water quality. Each closure reminds me that nature can only absorb and clean a limited amount. By our carelessness in handling the byproducts of civilization, we poison our own nest.

The wind is picking up with strong gusts rattling my windows and drainpipes. A flock of gulls glides by with outstretched wings motionless, as up drafts carry them sharply skyward. Two Brown Pelicans soar, straight-winged as if frozen in space and quickly disappear from sight. So, not all birds are hiding, some are braving the storm.

Later, as the sky begins to clear, I watch a young Black-crowned Night Heron looking very large and awkward as it roosts in a neighbor's tree. Its yellow feet and legs clutch a small branch as it shifts around looking as if it is trying to get comfortable. In my line of sight as I watch the heron, I can also see a sculpture in my secret garden often used as a roost by a Red-tailed Hawk. The hawk is very patient and will sit statue-like for hours waiting for a chance at a meal. Usually he hunts lizards and small birds from his elegant perch and I have to clean up clumps of feathers and little bloody piles of unrecognizable remains from the sculpture's top. I don't like having him raid my garden sanctuary, but I do like seeing him and being assured that nature is still somewhat balanced even in the middle of a neighborhood with houses and paved streets. The hawk is somewhere else today.

With a clear sky after the rain abates and the smell of damp earth strong in my nostrils, I finally have a chance to head for the beach. It is afternoon and since I usually walk in the morning, things seem strange, slightly off kilter. As I head across the fields, the afternoon sun is at my back instead of shining in my eyes, giving me a new sense of place. Bird sounds fill the fresh, rain-sifted air. Little chirps and twitters in the bushes make me look for flashes of color, but all I see are small brown birds perched in the remains of last year's Dill weed.

A hummingbird atop a Coyote Bush turns its head just enough to catch a sun ray on its throat and throw a red sequined light at me. Another hummingbird reflects only an iridescent green back. A small fluffy gray bird preens its feathers while perched atop a park trail sign. With a gentle breeze ruffling its head feathers, it takes on a jaunty, tousled look, like a rogue playboy set apart from the other birds spaced evenly on the wire fence top. Spider webs in the grass glisten with beads of moisture left from the rain. Their perfectly woven center funnels stand ready to capture the unwary insect.

A raven's hoarse caw ushers me along the path to the beach, but my shoes are already soaking and make squeaking sounds with each step I take on the wet ground. I think I have sopped up the moisture underfoot as well as the spirit of the day and I need go no further on my beachwalk.

The birds have come out of their rain-sheltered hiding places and I have left the shelter and comfort of my home to bask with them in the sunlight so welcome after a stormy morning. It is enough for today.

Western Gnatcatcher, *Polioptila caerulea*, a protected species due to habitat loss.

72

Fragments
assembling a beach quilt

"Let your hook be always cast;
in the pool where you least expect it,
there will be a fish."

Ovid

Soft moisture-laden air swirls off the sea and rises to scale the bluffs as a steady breeze blows inland. Showers are predicted by noon, but for now a thick overcast blocks the rising sun, painting the day in shades of pewter and steely-gray. Intense waves hit the shore in short intervals, sometimes washing high up the beach. The solid rock understructure of the shore, usually blanketed with several feet of sand, lies exposed and raw.

With so much of the sand washed away, a common winter occurrence, I find it takes concentration and balance to walk on the remaining layers of cobbles. So I pick my way carefully along, eyes glued to the ground in search of solid footing. A bit of bright color in the pebbly debris catches my eye and I pick up a piece of broken pottery, a triangular wedge of white decorated with a green ribbon and leaf border. Looks like part of a plate, I think, as I place the fragment in my pocket to carry home and add to other pieces of pottery and glass I have collected from my beachwalks. Why do these small fragments intrigue me? Is it because their colors remain true even after long periods of burial in the sands, or could it be the mystery behind each small artifact that attracts me?

I was first drawn to pottery shards on a trip through the Southwest where I visited ancient Anasazi Indian sites littered with pieces of broken clay bowls and pots, all from centuries ago. The strength of the ceramic material allowed them to lie among stones and dirt for hundreds of years, and yet retain their earthen shades of terra cotta, gray, charcoal and white. Corrugated surface designs made from thumb imprints and tiny, fine line painting gave each fragment an individual personality and special beauty. I imagined I could feel the life of the shard as I placed my thumb into the thumbprint of the potter who worked the clay. I studied each element of painted line and pictured the difficulty of executing such fine detail. Occasionally I was further rewarded with an additional artifact, such as a flaked stone tool or the carved bone bead on top of an ant hill, where ants had left it after clearing out their underground cavity.

Pencil sketches of Southwest Anasazi pottery shards with painted designs. The Anasazi lived in the four corners area of the American West and disappeared around 1,300, A.D.

Fret design. A typical version of this ancient motif

74

But s h a r d s always gave me the greatest excitement. From then on I was hooked on the beauty and mystery of these small remnants of a civilization existing long before my time.

The pieces of pottery I find on the beach are not ancient like Anasazi shards, but they still hold a fascination worth exploring. Broken yellow and blue tiles, terra cotta chunks from clay flower pots, a blue willow patterned tea cup section, numerous flowered plate shards, half a milk glass jar incised with an ancient fret design; these are my twentieth century pottery shards. Fragments with stories to tell of people and events. Some are yesterday's castoffs, but others may date back to the original Japanese agricultural community that existed at Crystal Cove before the 1920's beach cottages were built.

With each new remnant of clay, porcelain and glass, I find, my desire heightens to know how this fragment ended up on the beach. If only it were possible to unearth the story, the path that brought this artifact to its sandy resting place among sea-scoured pebbles and beach debris. Some pieces have little to distinguish them other than color and I cannot begin to guess about their origins or the object of which they were once a part. Others hold more clues for speculation, like the milkglass jar fragment with its fret design, a variation evolved from motifs used during Prehistoric times. I wonder, did it hold face cream, ointment, powder, medicine, and why did the manufacturer choose a 6,000 year old design for its decoration?

While it may not be known by the name, fret, most people would easily recognize this much used motif. Variations were incised into utensils and weapons by hands of people in the Stone Age. The Greeks and Romans used it as a border in floor mosaics and on painted pottery. It was chiseled into lintels of buildings and painted on walls in Pompeii. In North America, early Native Americans painted versions of it on their pottery, and today's Southwest Indians continue its use on ceramics, as well as baskets and rugs. And now, a pottery fragment found on the beach with that same design incised into the glass, confirms the fret's place in the 20th century just as surely as it belongs to all of history. Silently, it links generation to generation and ties civilizations together through their use of a universal pattern.

Plate with green ribbon and leaf design.

75

On this misty morning my hand closes around the plate shard in my pocket and I realize it is much more than a mere piece of broken pottery. It represents a portion of a life, and suddenly, I realize my life is a collection of fragments. A series of unrelated activities makes up my day moving from one purpose to another. The phone rings with messages that have nothing to do with what I am engaged in at the time. Elements of my life as wife, mother, friend, interact in bits and pieces to become a whole life. There are those who know me only by one of my aspects, a fragment of the whole me, just as I know the plate fragment, only from one broken piece with a small portion of design. I can only guess at the rest of the pattern. My closest friends have fragments of their lives they keep to themselves and I have fragments I do not share, but most of our aspects have a commonality that makes us similar, much like the universality of the fret design.

I sometimes think of fragmentation as negative, but if I could find and put all of my life fragments together at one time, the complexity of my being would be overwhelming. So I deal with them one at a time in the same way I sort my beach fragments, placing them in groups and categories that I can handle. There are shells, pottery shards, beach glass, sealife, driftwood, plants, bones, and the list continues to include experiences such as rainy days and whale sightings. There is pleasure for me in all of my beach fragments, each piece contributing to the whole. Researching any one expands my knowledge and gives meaning to the time spent on my beachwalk.

On a recent trip to Oregon, I hiked out to Clatsop Spit to see the remains of the Peter Iredale, a 1906 shipwreck. After nearly a hundred years of battering by sea and wind, there is only a fragment of structural steel protruding from the sandy strand. But that fragment keeps the memory of the ship fresh and meaningful. So fragments, while small in size, may be very large in representation and remembrance.

I think about pioneer women who used fragments of cloth to make quilts. Each piece of material had a history. A bit of worn out dress, a child's outgrown clothes, bright color swatches traded with a friend or neighbor, memories lovingly quilted together to form a warm, serviceable and meaningful cover, a blanket with history as well as purpose. The sewing of the quilt, itself, was a shared activity.

I think of the fragments I collect on my beachwalks as shards melding together to form my beach quilt. They are pieces of experiences broken and scattered, of pain and uncertainty, of adventures and joy and, most of all, they are reminders of a love that pervades life at its worst moments as well as at its best. As my collection of beach fragments grows and is stitched together with insights and relationships, I grow. But unlike a cloth quilt, my beach quilt is forever in the making, a continuous process that is ever rewarding and always hopeful. Today I go home with a new fragment in my pocket, and some new ideas to connect with the past while I piece together the present.

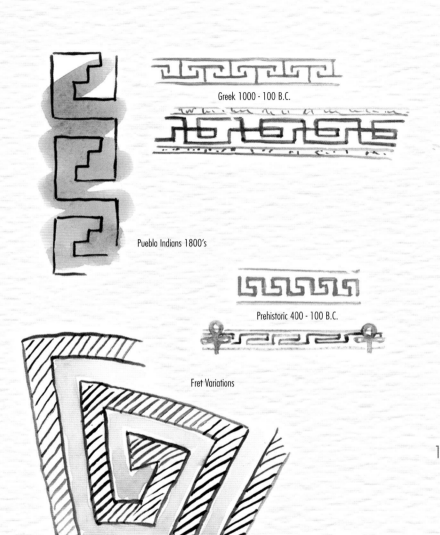

Greek 1000 - 100 B.C.

Pueblo Indians 1800's

Prehistoric 400 - 100 B.C.

Fret Variations

Pima Indian Basket 1800 - 1900

Greek Terra Cotta

1990 Milk glass jar fragment found on beach

Anasazi Bowls 1200 - 1300 A.D.

Small Disasters
sharing a common fate

"Who hears the fishes when they cry?"
Henry David Thoreau

I always look forward to my morning excursions on the beach, never knowing what new discovery will pique my curiosity. Crossing the fields on the path to the ocean, filled with eager anticipation, I breathe in the crisp sea-scented air as the thunder of booming surf blots out all other sounds. A quick scramble down a rock-strewn drainage path takes me to damp, soft-packed sand, where clumps of tangled seaweed scattered along the wide beach look like piles of raked debris on a sandy yard. It is late summer and I quickly see it has been a disastrous time for small sea life. In the masses of seaweed left behind by the receding tide are sad little reminders, proof of the overwhelming power the ocean holds within its tidal waters.

I pick up a keyhole limpet lying upside down, beached like a Lilliputian whale. I can't tell if it is still alive. Its soft under parts, a pink foot and black mantle, are exposed and beginning to desiccate in the weak early morning sun. But if there is any chance it can survive, I want to save it. All of the keyhole limpets in my shell collection are empty shells found on the beach, the living snail long gone. Today's limpet is one of the few I have come across with the snail still attached, somewhat like a tiny leg-less turtle covered with only the top half of its shell. Until I learned about keyhole limpets, I thought a snail was something black and slimy and coiled. Now I know a snail can also be pink and attached to one side of a flattened oval disk with a hole in the center.

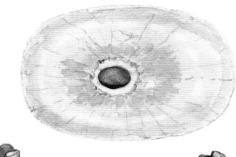

I carry the limpet in my hand to a deep tide pool and place it on an underwater rock, hoping it still has life and the ability to fasten down securely in order to withstand heavy wave action. It probably doesn't and that's why it washed up on shore, but I can't help at least giving it a chance. I intend to check on my way home to see if it has revived.

I walk past three sea hares, all obviously dead, their stiff little bodies resembling tar balls lying in the swash line. I read once that if every sea hare egg survived and grew into adulthood, laying more eggs that survived, it would take only a few weeks to cover the entire earth with sea hares. While they are simple, defenseless animals and no threat to man, a world populated with mostly black, squishy, slow-moving creatures looking a lot like foot-long snails would not be my choice. In spite of this weird statistic, I still rescue their orange spaghetti-like egg masses stranded on the beach. I always pick up the soft, wet strings of eggs and return them to tide pools, hoping they will have a chance to hatch. I think Mother Nature wouldn't resent a little help here and there, considering how much damage we generally do to her world.

Once I was delighted to came upon a bright orange sea hare egg mass just a few feet from one colored a brilliant purple. I had never before seen the purple clusters, which I finally realized represent a different species of sea hare. But it was the contrast of colorful orange and purple next to each other on the tan sand that created a sight I treasure and do not expect to see again.

Purple Olive Shells and Great Keyhole Limpet - underside: Great Keyhole Limpet, *Megathura crenulata,* ranges from Monterey California to Mexico. It can attain a length of 4 inches. Inside is grayish white and polished.

80

Still another sea hare lies directly in my path and this one looks alive, so it must have been beached very recently. Its head has two small projections that are really antennae, but look like ears and there are ruffles on its back that can stand up or lie flat. When a sea hare moves, it seems to have no bones, so it can take a variety of shapes, none of which looks like anything except some amorphous black mass. As I carry the sea hare back to its home in the tide pools, it flows over the edge of my hand like soft jelly. I have to keep pushing it back onto my palm, so it won't ooze off as I walk. Placing it in the water, where there is shelter under a ledge, I watch as the little creature points its head forward and begins a slow crawl to safety.

Statistically the California Black Sea Hare has the potential of reaching a length of thirty inches, but I've never seen one larger than about sixteen. It's a good thing this little one fit in one hand because there is no way I'm going cradle a thirty incher in my arms and carry it back to the sea.

Beached Keyhole Limpets, sea hares, and sea hare egg masses, these are a few of the small disasters of the beach. Though they are hardly small to the creatures who are the ones caught in the grips of displacement and death. But they are small in comparison to the destruction brought by huge disasters, like floods, droughts or deadly storms.

Small is only an adjective of comparison; it does not mean that something doesn't matter. Each small life and death is important and noteworthy. Each has some meaning and place in the order of things.

Shakespeare put it this way, "The sense of death is most in apprehension, and the poor beetle that we tread upon feels a pang as great as when a giant dies." So, death hits all. While I know I don't understand the whole process and meaning of life and death, I do know I can at least view it with reverence and respect and at times offer help or aid to a suffering fellow dweller on this planet. There are those who criticize or make fun of anyone who values the life or comfort of living things other than humans. But having sympathy for small creatures doesn't diminish in any way what I feel for those of my own species. I realize that I, too, will participate in the process of dying. My hope is that there is someone with me in my last moments who cares and tries to ease my pain.

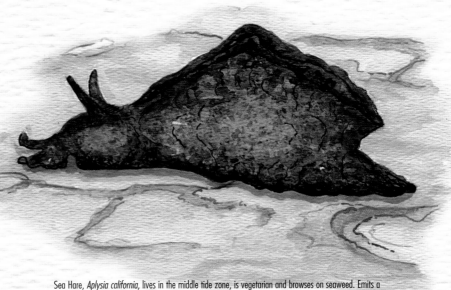

Sea Hare, *Aplysia california*, lives in the middle tide zone, is vegetarian and browses on seaweed. Emits a deep purple ink for protection when disturbed and lays eggs in long orange strings that resemble spaghetti.

I began my beachwalk today expecting cheerful sights and discoveries. But instead the morning has been dominated by a more somber tone, a sense of the fragility of life leading to thoughts of my own mortality. The beach is a natural organization, so it shows things as they are, the playing out of life and death with no favorites. I may not want to think about death or look at dead birds and stiffened sea hares decaying on the sand, but this morning I have no choice. I have to view reality on the beach and let it color my idealized concept of my special place. I acknowledge that though reality may hurt a bit or a lot, still, it makes me think and that's how I become a more balanced person. For that I am grateful.

While my encounters today focus on death I am not depressed. The beach with its freshness of air and water and sand reminds me, as well, of life and beauty. Colors and scents shout about living and make me feel like rejoicing

rather than mourning. Reminders of death imposed upon the beach's vibrant atmosphere, while touching and sad, present a natural balance I seldom see in my daily routines. Our society is organized to keep death and pain out of the public eye and most likely that is best, I think, or it could become overwhelming.

I pick up my beach pack and head for home so engrossed in my thoughts and my attempts to place lasting meaning on my morning of small disasters, I forget to check on the keyhole limpet I rescued to the tide pool. Perhaps it is better not knowing if it survived, so I can think of it as another life saved. If I count one keyhole limpet and one sea hare I can begin my day by believing I diminished the morning's small disasters by at least two.

Great Keyhole Limpet, *Megathura crenulata,* is mostly flat, but slightly rounded at center opening. Strong radiating lines and concentric growth rings decorate the top side of the shell.

Purple Olive Shells, *Olivella biplicata,* are about one inch high and highly polished. They range in color from deep purple to nearly white.

Scraper
a signpost from the past

"Every generation enjoys the use of a vast hoard bequeathed to it by antiquity, and transmits that hoard, augmented by fresh acquisitions, to future ages."

Thomas Macaulay

As I walk along the edge of the bluff just north of a deep arroyo that drains to the beach, I notice a stone with a wavy edge barely poking out of the ground near my feet. After some hard kicking with the heel of my shoe, the small gray rock loosens from its earthen bed. Had it not been for last night's downpour eroding the hard packed sand, exposing the layer below, the stone would still be cemented in place by natural forces, hidden from my view. As I brush away its encrusted dirt with my sleeve, I know I have found a treasure.

Looking closely at the gray stone in my hand, my heart beats a little faster. I feel certain this is a prehistoric artifact, a lithic, a stone tool shaped by human hands. The man-made flaked edge along one side is so sharp it nearly cuts me as I carefully test it with my thumb. The thick, opposite end fits comfortably into my palm. I am holding an ancient tool shaped for cutting and scraping, most likely made by early Native Americans who lived along this coast. The excitement of touching an object crafted by someone hundreds, perhaps thousands of years ago, races through me. I want to know more about this morning's discovery. But for now, all I do is tuck the tool safely into my pocket for later reflection and continue into the rain-speckled morning.

Some days later when I take the stone to an archeologist for positive identification, he confirms my initial reaction. It is, indeed, a lithic, an artifact from another civilization. He

Native American artifact,
quartzite scraper or denticulated flake knife.
Found on edge of the coastal terrace above the beach after a rain.

informs me that this two inch by three inch piece of finely grained quartzite, technically called a flake-knife or denticulated scraper, may have originated in a 4,000-year old campsite located about 200 yards upcoast from where I found it. The site has been identified and studied, but is now covered over with the grass and sand traps of Pelican Hills golf course.

I feel privileged to hold this tool as I imagine the others before me who have gripped the same stone, their damp palms leaving salty sweat on gray rock as they labor over daily chores. Much of what we know about these early people comes from analyzing their trash heaps, called middens. Abalone, snail and mussel shell fragments along with small animal bones provide information about their diet. Stone tools, grinding stones and beads made from Olivela shells found in the screens of archaeologists as they sift the soil, provide other clues about the life of these ones of the past.

Further research on the ancient people who camped on top of this bluff tells me they were seasonal inhabitants, as were those who flocked to the area earlier in my own century. Corona del Mar, where I live, was a summer destination for residents of Los Angeles and Pasadena in the 1940's and 1950's. Many of the houses were originally built as second homes and used only during the summer. For the first native inhabitants of this shore, a seasonal home providing sufficient shelter during the mild summer months was little more than a framework of sticks covered with tule reeds.

While historical fact confirms the existence of people thousands of years ago living where I now live, finding and holding one of their tools helps me to feel this knowledge. As I grasp the sturdy quartzite scraper, I merge with the past, becoming an extension of human habitation along these shores. Someone, many lifetimes before me, sat upon this same bluff top and looked across the ocean as I do now. She, too, must have

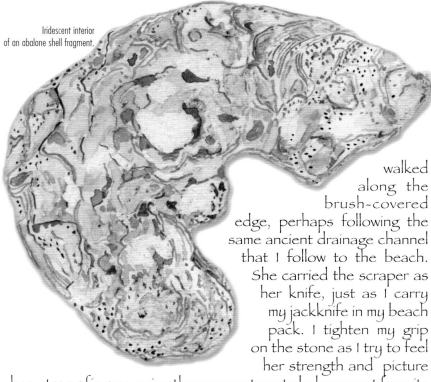

Iridescent interior
of an abalone shell fragment.

walked along the brush-covered edge, perhaps following the same ancient drainage channel that I follow to the beach. She carried the scraper as her knife, just as I carry my jackknife in my beach pack. I tighten my grip on the stone as I try to feel her strength and picture her strong fingers using the scraper to cut abalone meat from its shell. I see her kneeling as she fills the natural holes in the shell with beach tar. Placing the abalone in her new bowl, she follows the path back to her encampment to share her wealth. I smile as I think of how I, too, sometimes carry home an abalone shell. But mine is only an ornament and the abalone meat I eat comes from the market.

Slowly I begin to grasp the significance of her scraper in my hand. Four thousand years may separate us, but in ways that define us as human, our lives are the same. Blood types and skin color are of no importance to me. I see all humanity connected by a shared experience of existence.

To this day, the scraper that rose to the surface after its burial for so many years continues to touch my soul. It helps me find wholeness in the discovery of new things and the simple activity of my beachwalk. The scraper binds me to those who were here before and reaches out to touch those of the future. I see my children and grandchildren taking their places in the survival of mankind, wrapped in threads of continuity that give purpose and meaning to our lives. As individuals we have limited life expectancies, but as a part of our species we are eternal. The generations of humankind have no distinct beginning and no end. They are only signposts marking the progression from ancestors to inheritors who, in turn, become ancestors. With this scraper as a signpost, I find my place in time as an individual and my importance as a part of the whole.

Abalone shell fragments

Two views of a small Black Abalone, *Haliotis cracherodii*, the most abundant abalone on the California coast.

A food source for early people - Clumps of Blue Mussels fastened to rocks and seaweed with byssus threads. Pink Barnacles and small Rock Scallop attached to mussels.

Beach Glass
imperfections of time

*"It is good to have an end to journey towards;
but it is the journey that matters in the end."*

Ursula LeGuin

The beach is bathed in early morning halflight as the rising sun still hovers behind the eastern bluffs. A layer of puffy red-tinged clouds reflects hidden rays, soon to rise above the shadowy outcropping of land bordering the sea. Suddenly a brightness appears at the bluff top and the sun's rays shoot outward like an exploding firecracker. The quiet beach in my view bursts into a sparkling field of twinkling glitter as quartz crystals in the sand reflect newly emerging shafts of yellow light.

My eyes scan the expanse ahead, searching for bits of colorful beach glass brought to the surface by the outgoing tide. I hope to find small glass fragments of bright green, pale blue, brown and white nestled amongst earthy-toned pebbles and sand scoured clean by retreating waves. As I walk along, I am pulled towards a small glimmer of bottle-green flickering in the morning sunlight. I pluck the shiny shard from the sand and caress its smooth surface with my thumb. As I look at the fragment of broken glass so abraded that its original transparency is nearly opaque, its slick glossy surface transformed into a new and complex texture, I think of "touchstones," those small rocks that feel good to hold and stroke.

The Japanese have a reverence and a name, *wabi sabi,* for objects which have acquired imperfections and the patina of time. Beach glass fragments have *wabi sabi.* A shard of sharp glass with softness instilled by the scouring of sea and sand results in an object of sensual beauty. Time and tumbling have enriched them with a new and higher value.

On this morning, the waves have uncovered many pieces of beach glass and soon my pockets bulge with the weight of my findings and pull down the edges of my jacket, but I still bend to pick up one more piece. I tell myself I will stop collecting as soon as I find a fragment of cobalt blue, the rarest color of all. And as rarity breeds desire, I continue searching, but no blue appears.

I am not alone in my fascination with beach glass. Almost everyone I know who regularly frequents a beach will admit to a jar or two of the brightly colored fragments. I have seen these wave and sand-battered bits of colored glass fashioned into jewelry and displayed in an art museum. Recently I was shocked to see that boutiques were carrying scented, artificially created beach glass as potpourri for the home. While the glass was just as pretty, I felt betrayed by the display of a manufactured fake, made by machines and man rather than by waves and sand.

While I treasure these jewels of the beach, I am more intrigued with how a piece of broken glass becomes a beach treasure, of how transformation from a jagged shard to a lovely little gem takes place. By tumbling in waves and sand over time, sharp edges are ground into smooth curves, slick surfaces sanded to a soft texture, the original see-through quality permeated with a shadowy deepness.

Time is an important element in the process of creating beach glass just as it is in cementing relationships. Beach glass cannot be made overnight nor can lasting friendships be developed in a hurry. Both are part of a long process, and if they are true and real, cannot be quickly manufactured.

During our lifetimes there are events leaving us with sharp and jagged edges, but beach glass reminds us we don't need to stay that way. If we give the process a chance, let the pummeling and pounding of living give us new qualities, we can transform over time into something much better, our sharp edges gone, our surface no longer slick. By developing our deep inner color, we, too, can become jewels, like the beach glass.

With jars of beach glass standing on my patio, I was once tempted to find a use for it. So one year I made Christmas ornaments and boxes with lids using a hot glue gun to fuse the irregular pieces together. For myself I made a two-foot diameter sun disk, which I displayed on a Plexiglas stand so that light coming through it created a miniature stained glass window. Within two years every object I had so laboriously created had fallen apart. The hot glue, seemingly so sturdy, did not hold over time. The glue that binds together objects or relationships must be worthwhile in itself or ultimately the relationships will fail and the objects will fall apart like my glass boxes and ornaments.

Finally I found a better use for my beach glass. Outside of my studio window I created a glass garden of different colored concentric rings placed around a white quartz boulder. I placed a ring of white or colorless glass around the center stone, then pale blue, aqua, green and lastly brown. Each piece represents the effort of bending to the ground, a physical exercise of benefit to my body. Mentally, the pieces together represent a humbling acceptance of life's daily blows and blessings. The thousands of glass shards in my garden are a physical manifestation of the thousands of events impacting the person I have become, a daily reminder that the punches and hard knocks of life have their purposes.

My mother-in-law always said that as we get older, we become "more so." She meant that traits exhibited early in life in small ways become magnified as we allow them to surface more and more. Whether good or less desirable habits become dominant depends upon how we weather life's scouring. We all follow our own unique process of transformation from the way we were born to what we become. Each bit of buffeting leaves a mark. Together the marks shape a life. Like the beach glass, each of us has our own unique possibilities.

I return home with my pockets heavy with beach glass in various colors, but cobalt blue has eluded me this morning. I will add these shards to my glass garden and know that whatever the day holds for me, it is but a part of the shaping of myself, the sanding and smoothing of my jagged edges, the deepening of my soul.

Blue, green and red glass: Cobalt blue and red beach glass are rare. Glass is prohibited by law on California beaches.

Beach Huts
in the spirit of play

"The time you enjoy wasting is not wasted time."

Bertrand Russell

A low overcast hangs over the beach on this day in August. Without the warmth of the morning sun, I shiver in the crisp, damp air. If I quicken my step and swing my arms purposefully, I will generate more body heat, I think, as I hurry along the edge of the receding tide line. Ahead, a dark mass on the wide expanse of sand, catches my attention and I forget about the chill in the air as I approach the mysterious mound that wasn't there the last time I walked the beach. Finally, I am near enough to make out the outline of a hut that must have been built over the weekend and has survived the high tide.

The structure, made from various sized driftwood logs is square and rests over a shallow depression dug into the sand. To give more height to the interior, I think, as I peek through the doorway, framed with sturdy tree trunks bleached gray from sun and salt water. Cautiously, I step down the slanted, sand ramp and stand quietly inside, surveying the roof beams and wondering if they are safe. Driftwood pieces piled together, leaning on one another and held in place entirely by gravity seem unstable and dangerous. I picture the whole structure collapsing, burying me in a sandy grave where I might not be found for weeks. I quickly step back outside, feeling relieved. Looking at it from the beach, the roof beams seem quite secure and the whole structure reminds me of a log cabin lean-to our pioneer ancestors might have built as they crossed the country on their way West.

I compare today's hut with others I've seen during my beachwalks, and I realize it is much more elaborate and must be the result of a group effort. Over the years, of the hundreds of huts I've seen and photographed, each was a unique construction put together from whatever beach materials happened to be available at the time. Branches and tree trunks carried down rivers to the sea with every major rainstorm accumulate and provide the spark for building. It wouldn't be possible to construct two huts alike using natural driftwood, but some shapes occur more often than others. A teepee-like framework is the most common if there are long poles among the driftwood piles.

One of my favorite structures was rounded like an igloo and draped with seaweed, reminding me of ancient Siberian huts made from Wooly Mammoth bones. But the bones of this beach are of wood instead of calcium. Bleached gray driftwood, the scattered remains of living trees, stripped of skin and sinew and sun-dried clean, take the place of Mammoth ribs and tusks. Some huts are simply a hodgepodge of sticks and sand, but elaborate or simple, each is a work of art, an assemblage of found objects put together with the joy of creating, blurring the line between art and playfulness.

The simplest type of beach hut is a teepee-like structure.

There is a universal urge to build shelter, even when it is play shelter. No one is too old to play house. Even Marie-Antoinette had small outbuildings built at Versailles and entertained Louis XVI in cottages decorated with furniture made from reeds and branches. Old English gardens of wealthy people often contained follies or structures that were completely whimsical.

Here on the beach, the abundance of raw material makes building a play house almost irresistible. The huts are similar to sandcastles in that an amusing half-dream edifice is constructed. Except the huts are one step closer to reality in that they can actually be entered. I see huts adorned with draped seaweed, outfitted with toothbrushes and cups, pretty shells and rocks, all kinds of plastic items, parts of toys, flowers, all combed from the flotsam of the swash line.

Before this area became Crystal Cove State Park, the beach huts were built mostly by surfers for shelter from sun and wind, and, I suppose, there was also an element of staking a claim to the beach. In those days the huts were a communal activity and lasted through whole seasons with repairs made when needed by anyone who happened to be around. I liked those structures the best and felt a loss when storms or high tides took them down.

The hut on today's swath of sand reminds me of one afternoon on the beach with my husband and three grandsons. I found myself engaged in the same process of building a hut, I had so often observed with others. We built a lean-to out of driftwood. The heavy framework was set up by my husband while each grandson dragged building material from further and further away after the nearby piles were depleted. As they worked at setting sticks in place and heaping sand upon the seaweed roof, their delight and

total commitment to the project reflected in their contented faces. When the hut was eventually deemed finished, the two older boys placed branching sticks on either side of the entrance, simulating decorative trees, while the younger one scooped out a path leading to the doorway.

A week later our beach hut was still there and as I walked by on a Sunday afternoon, a father with two young sons had adopted it and were busily arranging and rearranging the driftwood pieces we had collected. The unspoken tradition of preserving and adding to existing structures in the spirit of play continues, I thought. Our hut had become their hut. I smiled to myself about our shared experience. My secret, I thought, as I passed by, a stranger they barely noticed.

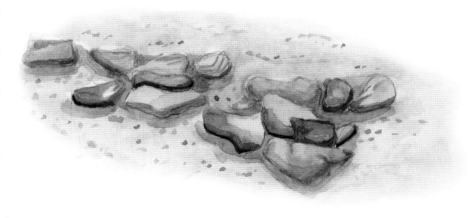

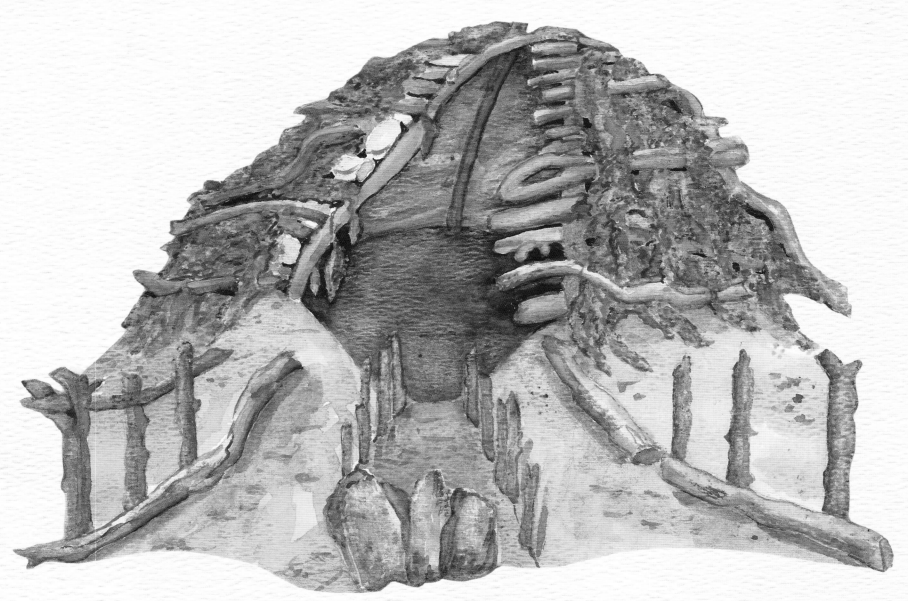

Heavy bleached tree limbs at the entrance of this beach hut remind me of ancient huts built of fossilized Mammoth tusks in cold climate regions.

Song
music is born inside

"Does the song of the sea end at the shore or in the hearts of those who hear it?"
Kahlil Gibran

The tide, lower than I have seen it for days, leaves little pools of sea water caught within rocky depressions and swirled-out sand basins. Heaps of shells and smooth, sea-rounded pebbles blanket parts of the rocky coastal shelf usually underwater and swept by waves. As I amble slowly from one beckoning mound to another, looking for glistening green and white beach glass or a perfect shell specimen, my heart sings. It sings the song of the beach, the song of strong waves and warm wind and calling birds and anticipation of the day's discoveries.

I would love to burst into song out of sheer joy on this beautiful morning, but I can't carry a tune and when I try, I am so flat and off key I break out in laughter at how bad I sound. I hear the notes so clearly in my head, but I am unable to reproduce them aloud. When I was a teenager I sang in the church choir and the school choir since no willing volunteer was ever excluded from either group. If I had someone with a strong alto voice standing next to me, I could follow reasonably well adding my voice to the whole without embarrassment. But singing solo was never an option even by myself for my own enjoyment.

So I listen to music rather than make music. Some operatic arias are so beautiful, they choke up my throat and bring tears to my eyes. *Nessun dorma* from Puccini's Turandot never fails to move me past tears and into euphoria. That anyone could conceive and perform music so moving is an absolute marvel to me. Some popular songs give me a good feeling or remind me of happy times or special occasions. "Pomp and Circumstance" and Handel's "Wedding March" automatically summon up deep emotions through associations with the major events they represent.

Along with not being able to sing I don't play any musical instrument either. I haven't touched the piano since grade school, when, after five years of piano lessons and torturous practice sessions, I succeeded only as far as playing easy church hymns if they didn't have too many sharps or flats. So I don't count that.

There is, however, music living in my soul I alone can hear. This inner music floats my emotions to the surface when experiencing orange-mauve sunsets and glacier-wrapped mountains. This is the music that brings tears to my eyes when watching breaching whales and gracefully leaping dolphins. This is music from a source within me and like all powerful music, it has an effect beyond words.

Over many years of beachwalking, I have come to recognize the song within my soul as I become one with the sand and sea. Rainy, overcast, fog-filled days send a more somber tune through my being than the joy-filled melodies of clear, sunny, cloudless skies. Through time I've learned to love the many moods of different weather along my strip of coastline and to revel in each change as it settles along the shore. I compare my beach moods with the many moods of life and only wish my heart could sing as well at each new stage I experience.

It is so easy to become comfortable in routine and to fight change. But I am learning to embrace a shifting, a variation of how I must live and to recognize its new value. At one time, I loved running on the beach, but when my knees gave out and I was no longer able to place that kind of strain on them, I was devastated. Only slowly did I begin to accept walking in place of running. In time

Norris Top shells: These small whorled shells have the spiral shape of large shells that hold the song of the sea when held against one's ear.

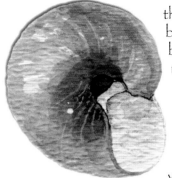

the walk became normal and now I love my beachwalk and realize how much I missed before. As I move at a slower speed, my eyes take in new details, like tiny periwinkle snails covering shore rocks, the intricate structure of beached seaweed, bird tracks embroidering the sand. All would have been missed during a run. I have gained a whole new world through a shift in my physical ability. Having a limitation on how my body performs has helped me to see the importance of appreciating each day and whatever it may hold for me, to savor each moment and look for pleasure in the smallest of things, a tiny flower, a fresh scent, a scurrying shore crab, sea grass on rock, quiet time and most of all to listen to the song of the sea as I perceive it from within me.

On days when the tide is so high it covers the entire swath of beach sand and laps against the base of the bluffs, I walk above on the coastal terrace. The disappointment of missing the beach is soon gone as I am rewarded with little white-tailed rabbits crossing my path to hide motionless in clumps of yellow Bush Sunflower and orange Deerweed. A roadrunner may scoot quickly ahead and disappear into the saltbush. The kitten-like mewing of the California Gnatcatcher blends with the melodious notes of a Meadowlark. Little brown unidentified birds line up and "cheep-cheep" on a wire fence top. Two lone quail, with their jaunty top knots silhouetted against the asphalt path, dash into the underbrush for cover as they continue their morning scratchings for food. On the bluff top my heart's song echoes the stirrings of small furry creatures, twittering feathered songsters and vibrantly colored flowers. It is a song different from one down near the water with crashing waves and windswept sand.

Operculum

On my walk today, the orchestra of the beach fills the air around me and makes me use my ears to listen with my soul. I hear the drum roll of pounding surf, a beat that sets the pace for today's symphony. Filling in the background, sparkling water sweeps in and out of tide pools presenting a soft timpani. Waves with five foot curls crash like cymbals as they hit the sand with intense force. An unrelenting sea wind fills my ears with the softness of violins, while gulls interject high pitched soprano notes as they argue over a scrap of seaweed. Even a ground squirrel's staccato squeak and the harsh caws of a crow riding thermals above the cliffs, contribute to the medley of sounds, a concerto of ocean and shore.

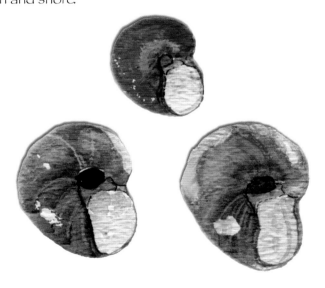

Graduated sizes of Norris Top Shells, *Norrisia Norrisii*, with operculum, the trapdoor closing that protects the pale red snail inside. All of the Norris Top Shells I've found have been empty.

97

These melodies are the essence of the beach. Combined with other sights, sounds and scents, they cocoon around me defining my place and sense of who I am. And each day they play a new composition. This is how I hear the music of the beach. This is how I hear the music within my soul. This is how I sing.

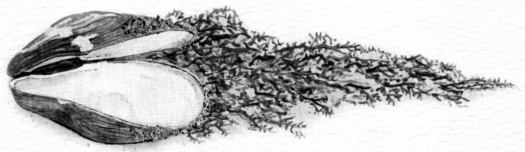

Horse Mussel, *Modiolus modiolus,* can grow to 7 inches. Found worldwide in northern seas.

Driftwood
searching for character

"Character is formed in the stormy billows of the world"
Goethe

Looking down at the ocean from the bluff top, I watch as waves rush up the slanted shore, bounce off the foot of the cliff and spill their energy with the receding flow. When the tide is at its highest like this, the beach is gone, submerged for a while under a cleansing sheet of foaming water. So this morning I stay on the coastal terrace above the beach and follow asphalt park paths lined with aromatic sage and tall clumps of saltbush.

When I reach Pelican Point, I decide to make one more try at gaining access to the beach below. Following the path as it curves around the hillside, I pause at a bench rest spot and read the story of driftwood on the park interpretive sign. Driftwood, it tells me, begins as trees far from the beach and through forces of weather is carried many miles down rivers to the sea where ocean currents and waves deposit the floating wood onto shore. Then over time, sun and saltwater bleach it to a silvery gray.

I think about the many remnants of bleached and abraded driftwood I've dragged home over the years. Most pieces ended up in my secret garden nestled in between plants or displayed in half-hidden nooks. Fat chunky stumps, twisted branches, and gnarled root masses lie under orange-flowered lantana and poke out from under drifts of blue Vinca. One of my favorites picked up from the beach near my house is a driftwood tree trunk riddled with holes, some still filled with acorns. It was once the storage cupboard for an Acorn Woodpecker's winter supply of nuts. I wonder and worry a little about the fate of the woodpecker who lost its carefully stored winter food supply.

Woodpeckers are not indigenous to my yard, but about a hundred miles away in the San Bernardino Mountains they are common. While hiking there, I have seen clusters of tall pine trees, their trunks polka-dotted with holes made by these birds. Each hole is pecked into the tree bark and filled with an acorn. The birds do not ever intend to use the nut as food. Instead they eat the worm that develops in the acorn over the winter.

It is from this same forest and others like it that storm water carries fallen trees and brush down the Santa Ana River to empty into the sea just a few miles upcoast from Crystal Cove. So I know my driftwood stump decorated with woodpecker holes came many miles before it landed on my shore.

As I continue down the path at Pelican Point, I see the high tide has not covered this raised shelf of fractured rock. It is inundated, instead, with cobbles and beds of driftwood. So I must pick my way through stacks of rubble, an estimated 1,800 tons of wood debris for this winter alone. Due to a peculiar meteorologic condition called El Niño, the Spanish name for Christ Child, weather around the globe was upset resulting in warmer water and more rain to our shores. With the rain, comes driftwood. Since I have so much to choose from, surely I can find a nice piece to take home from this morning's walk.

I step carefully over piles of bleached gray sticks, scanning the collections of jumbled wood and organic material for anything that looks unusual. I ignore straight branches and look for gnarled and twisted limbs with knots or prominent wood graining. I do not know what I'm looking for, but I will recognize the beauty of a gracefully twisted branch stripped of its bark and beach sanded to a sensual smoothness, when I see it.

I remember the first bit of driftwood I brought home. It was years ago when I came across a small sinuously curved stick that reminded me of a snake. I hate snakes, but I was drawn to the mellow red-brown color of this wood fragment. At home, I shaped a head and tail, sanded it to bring out the grain, and planned to give it to my daughter, Holly, who had a pet grass snake when she was a teenager. Her snake owning period was traumatic for me because the snake always got out when she wasn't around and I was the one who had to trap it in a closet or drawer until she got home from school. I certainly wasn't going to touch it and I knew it would drive me wild if it was loose somewhere in the house.

But before I was able to give Holly her "snake," I began to see other snake sticks on my beachwalks and soon I had quite a collection captured in the garage. Inspiration hit me one day and I got out my paints and colored all my snakes with whimsical non-snake colors. It turned out to be a kind of therapy for me, as I worked at making friendly creatures out of shapes that otherwise repulsed me. All my friends ended up with a "snake" for Christmas that year. Some I kept as decorations in my own house to remind me that after handling and painting snaky shapes, I felt much friendlier towards the real thing. Now I see a snake and look at it with curiosity instead of automatic revulsion. Never could I have guessed, when I picked up that first driftwood stick on the beach, that it would have such a positive effect upon my life.

Today I am trying to figure out what it is that makes a gnarled piece of driftwood full of imperfections, so appealing to me. Is it the subtlety of grain or color or tortured shape that turns an old piece of wood into a thing of beauty? As my eyes search the piles of beach debris for the unusual, it dawns on me that it is the complexity of all these elements together shaping each individual piece, that captures my interest. Wind and weather directing its growth from a tiny seed to its development into a tree, its journey from the soil of its birth to its beach resting place, and finally, its destiny as firewood, ornament, garden decor, or trash to be hauled away.

As I continue my search for interesting wood formations, my mind wanders and I begin to compare the imperfections of wood to gnarled and aging people. They, like the driftwood, have been changed by experiences and time, but have survived with scars of remembrance. Slowly I realize it is the development of character that appeals to me and ultimately becomes a kind of beauty. It is character I'm looking for in the driftwood, character developed over a long journey, just as I look for character in people who have lived full and challenging lives, molding the clay of experience into living artifacts of lasting value.

Age lines and wrinkles on a human face, like knots and burls on driftwood, add to the beauty of the individual as manifestations of character. Just as driftwood attains its mellow patina with time, those people who age with an inner beauty and exceptional character take on a patina setting them apart from the ordinary. Mother Teresa who comforted the sick in the slums of India is probably the best example, but we all know someone in our own neighborhood who is noteworthy for caring and performing unexpected acts of kindness.

Natural changes produce attractive and collectible driftwood. As my own natural changes take place, I must remember they, too, can become attributes of character. Looking at my own knots and imperfections, my wrinkles and lines, I realize that while I may not like them, they, too, add to my identity as an individual.

My search for a piece of driftwood with character ends as I find a sturdy forked tree branch, gracefully curved, smooth, already stripped of its bark. It can serve as a perching place for birds dining at the feeder outside my studio window. With a firm grip I balance the heavy branch on my shoulder and struggle up the ramp to the coastal terrace as I head for home. While passing my neighbors houses, I feel a little self-conscious and silly with a cumbersome piece of driftwood slung over my back. Then I remember, it doesn't matter if I look strange marching down the street carrying a big tree limb. I'm just building character.

Driftwood is frequently very esthetic in shape, color and texture.

Deer
powerboat guardians

"We wander, but in the end there is always a certain peace in being what one is,--"
Ugo Betti

My good friend, Doretta, is walking with me this morning and while crossing the coastal terrace on our way to the beach, we spot a Tarantula Hawk crawling along the edge of the path. We stop to look more closely at this big black wasp with rusty-orange wings and wonder if it is out hunting or if it has already found a Tarantula to prey upon. Tarantula Hawks have a unique arrangment for feeding their young. It begins with finding a Tarantula spider, paralyzing it with a bite, laying an egg on the immobile spider's abdomen and finally, burying the Tarantula alive. The spider, conscious, but unable to move becomes the food source for the Tarantula Hawk's egg. When it hatches into a worm-like larva it eats the paralyzed spider alive.

I'm not sure what Mother Nature was thinking when she came up with this neat little arrangement for nourishing Tarantula Hawk young, but it seems extremely cruel to me. To be buried alive and eaten little by little while in a conscious but paralyzed condition is not my idea of how things should happen. However, I have a tendency to idealize nature, so I need only remind myself of this strange arrangement in the Tarantula Hawk's reproductive cycle, for a return to the reality that nature is neither kind nor cruel. It is what it is.

We leave the Tarantula Hawk to its grisly work and descend the steps to the beach, where small sandpipers, their feet moving in fast clockwork unison, like tiny wind up toys, race back and forth with the ebb and flow of each wave. They live dangerously, always moving to safety a split second ahead of the incoming surge. How do they know when to scurry away from the advancing water? I watch the waves, trying to predict their flow onto the sand. I never get it right. Flows I think will go left, instead push right. I wouldn't make it as a sandpiper.

As we near the vintage beach houses at Crystal Cove, we spot a brown head bobbing in the surf. Thinking sea lion, we move closer and are surprised to see it is a deer swimming towards shore, a female since it has no antlers. Out beyond the surf line a power boat idles with people on board shouting and gesturing. Finally the deer reaches shallow water.

My pulse quickens as I watch a wave sweep the doe sideways onto the sand. She tries to stand, but the next wave pushes her feet askew and she is down again. She fights to right herself as each new wave throws her back into the roiling surf. Seeing her struggle against the power of the waves, I worry we will have to help her if she can't make it on her own and I know it would be very dangerous. Deer hooves are sharp and capable of cutting like knives. I fear she might not realize we are trying to help and we could be badly hurt if she fights us. But what choice would we have if the waves are too much for her.

She keeps trying and finally manages to stand upright on thin wobbly legs. She looks exhausted, but succeeds in taking a few unsteady steps onto the beach and out of the waves' reach. I breathe a sigh of relief, as she pauses, seems to catch her breath and slowly, tentatively makes her way inland, gaining a little more stability with each hesitant move forward. Doretta and I stand quietly, like statues, almost afraid to breathe for fear of frightening her. We don't talk or move until she has made her way up the brushy bank and disappeared behind the cottages.

A few days later, the local paper carried a story about the 100-pound mule deer. She was spotted by some boaters three miles offshore with a gathering of birds following as she plowed through the water. The boaters tried to turn the deer back to land and when that didn't work, they lassoed her, hauled her aboard, rode in close to shore and released her. The yelling we heard was the boaters trying to frighten her into swimming towards the beach and cheering when she made it. They were the heroes of the morning.

Several other times I have seen deer tracks in the sand and I always wonder why they would come to the beach. Certainly not for a drink, but then maybe they are seeking out salt from sea water or salt encrusted rocks. On the family farm in northern Minnesota, it was common for deer to come to the barnyard and lick the salt blocks put out for cows. When I asked the question of a park ranger, he said other deer have been seen swimming in the ocean and no one really knows why. They may simply be disoriented and swim out to sea, where chances are they will tire and drown. Sometimes people also head in the wrong direction and continue on instead of changing course. Some, like the deer, get help and are redirected for a new chance at life. Others are less fortunate and sink out of sight on their wrong way journey.

In my life there were times it was hard to know which way to go. I spent time floundering around trying to find the right road to take. Somehow I was lucky. There were power boat guardians to push me shoreward. A gentle word, inspiring moment, or scolding from a friend can change a course and make all the difference.

On the way back from our exciting morning of seeing the deer, I almost step on a Monarch butterfly lying in the swash line. Its vivid black and orange coloration contrasts strongly with light beach sand. Its wings are folded, and a narrow strip of sea grass is caught in its black thread like legs. Thinking I will use it as a subject for a painting, I carefully grasp its wings firmly between my thumb and forefinger, so the brisk breeze from the south will not blow it from my hand. I know it is too fragile to place in my beach pack, where it will be crushed.

Near the gate I spot a wonderful Wolf Spider in the center of its perfect web. I get out my camera to take its picture, and my friend, ever good-natured about helping me bring home my beach finds, takes the butterfly into her cupped hands to keep it out of the wind. After holding it for a few minutes, as I watch the spider, she says with surprise, "It's alive, I feel it tickling my fingers!"

The seemingly lifeless Monarch I'd snatched from the sand had, indeed, revived. Since the beach is not the usual environment for the Monarch, I make a carrier out of my hands and carefully transport the butterfly home to my yard, where I gently set it in a sheltered corner. The Monarch spends the rest of the morning testing its wings and moving around within the small wind-free area. I am concerned that I have hurt it while carrying it when I thought it was dead. I have heard that butterfly wings are coated with a powder that is necessary for flight and when rubbed off damages the wings.

When I check at noon, the Monarch is gone. I have to believe it recovered fully and flew away. I wish it had stayed in my garden, but just as I have my life patterns, I know Monarchs have migration routes and patterns their lives follow. I hope this straggler from its normal path found where it belongs and is doing what butterflies do. The deer we observed earlier was also out of her usual environment and I hope she was able to safely cross the highway and return to the brushy cover of the hillsides, back to her normal life.

I may not like it, but the Tarantula Hawk wasp with its system of using a live spider as food for its young, was also following its life pattern. Whether it is of nature's creatures or fellow humans, some life patterns are much more appealng than others. If I return to this earth in another form, please let me be the butterfly and not the Tarantula.

Monarch Butterfly entwined in strands of sea grass found lying in the swash line. Monarchs migrate thousands of miles every year. Their sole food source at one stage in life is milkweed.

Beachwalk Failure
cluttered thoughts intrude

"Our life is frittered away by detail. . . . Simplify, simplify!"
Henry David Thoreau

It is just past daybreak as I head across the coastal terrace wondering what new or interesting discovery awaits me on the wave swept, rock strewn shore below. The ground is damp with tiny beads of nighttime moisture still clinging to the tips of grasses and leafy edges of bushes lining my path. Among the dried twigs of a saltbush, a spider web is covered with dew and looks like a crystal lace doily crocheted of spun glass. The spider is hiding somewhere out of my sight. Perhaps it is sheltered under an umbrella-like leaf and remains dry and cozy and free of evening dew now settled on each tiny filament of its delicate, intricately woven web.

Clouds in shades of gray and mauve swirl slowly overhead in a milky sky, while on the ground a breeze from the south increases in strength as I descend the ramp to the beach. I walk into the wind feeling it rush across my face and neck. It roars past my ears muffling the boom of thundering surf. I am isolated in a cocoon of white noise created by the wind as it tears at my sweatshirt and whips past my cheeks. I feel alienated, like a foreign object set down in someone else's world.

Ordinarily, on my beachwalk, I become so much a part of the environment that time and purpose fade away as I wander free, existing only for the moment. But today is different as I trudge forward trying to clear my mind of yesterday's thoughts, to open a new page for what my beachwalk might uncover. I feel troubled by aftereffects from last night's dreams hanging in my consciousness and clinging to me just like the nighttime dew coats the morning ground. Though I can't remember any specific dream, vague images and unsettling feelings persist. I sometimes dream of needing to study for a test and not being able to find the textbook or the right classroom. Sometimes I'm trying to get dressed for a party and I can't find my clothes. I understand these are frustration dreams, but I don't even know what the frustration is. So I try to brush them away, to clear my mind, to

lose myself in the experience of the beach, to be unencumbered during the brief time of my beachwalk. Instead, my cluttered thoughts flutter in and around my consciousness like insects drawn to a light. I am here in body, but not in mind. I realize I am so bound by the sticky strands in the web of my daily life that no amount of mental flailing will free me. I can walk on the beach but I cannot escape today to my beachwalk world.

I begin to feel a slight mist on my face and hair and wonder if I will be rained on. There have been many mornings I left my house dry and came home damp and chilled from moisture unleashed by low clouds and morning fog, a typical weather forecast for the beach area. I stop to pick up a dead, but intact, purple crab, which I wrap in a plastic bag so I can store it in my freezer until I have a chance to capture its image with paper and paintbrush. My son teases me mercilessly about odd things I keep frozen. He jokes about his reluctance to retrieve anything from the freezer, since he is likely to find a dead bird or some slimy looking sea creature. He is right about his chances of finding a strange inedible item, but it is a convenient way for me to preserve specimens I want to paint. For several years, I actually collected dead birds for a professor at California State University Long Beach, whose students prepared them as specimens for an ornithology collection. It seemed right, somehow, to use a bird already dead by an accident of nature for an educational purpose to ultimately help the whole species.

Today as I walk, I scan the rough sea hoping for a glimpse of dolphins or maybe a spume of hot whale's breath above the whitecapped waves. Alternately, I search the sand at my feet for anything unusual. Nothing catches my interest and I find myself thinking about yesterday and planning my schedule for today, precisely what I don't want to intrude on my beachwalk. I realize I will receive very little mental renewal from this walk. I am walking on the beach, but I am not beachwalking.

Kelp Crabs live in kelp beds and are sometimes washed ashore.

So I move on feeling a little discontented and unsettled. I am reminded that as hard as I try, there are times when unwanted thoughts and musings take control, binding me in their net of turmoil for reasons I don't know or understand, and I am not strong enough to overcome their dominant influence.

As the wind diminishes, the slight mist turns into steady rain. I pull my sweatshirt hood over my head for protection. If only I could as easily pull down a shade to screen out unwanted, invading thoughts affecting my beachwalk on this damp, gray day. By the time I hurry back up the dry wash and across the fields at a half jog, half run, rain is hitting the ground in slanted sheets. When I arrive home wet and chilled, the only dry thing on me is the purple crab in its plastic bag for internment in my freezer.

After a warm shower and several hot cups of coffee, I think, even though my morning beachwalk failed in its concept of mental renewal, it was good for me to be reminded that I can learn from failure as well as success. Failure helps me more fully understand myself and admit to my weaknesses. It is not depressing to fail. It is merely another aspect of life. I smile as I mentally joke that I failed beachwalk 101 this morning. But why worry when I can enroll again tomorrow and hope for better success. I need only remember that like the tide-cleansed sand, tomorrow is a clean, new opportunity.

This California Blue Mussel has a colony of Goose-neck Barnacles, *Pollicipes polymerus,* living on it. The name comes from an old belief that geese hatched from them. The word "barnacle" probably referred to the medieval Latin word for goose, *"bernaca."*

110

Fossil Shells

messages in stone

"Maybe if I listen closely to the rocks
Next time, I'll hear something, if not
A word, perhaps the faint beginning of a syllable."

Phoebe Hanson

Yesterday and last night it rained. The tail end of a Pacific Northwest storm hit Southern California with welcome moisture after several months of drought. From the bluff top, I listen to thunderous booms of storm-generated waves pounding the coast. Down on the beach, the massive rock shelf of the shore swept bare of its usual blanket of sand, lies naked, exposed. The base layer of blue-gray rock, wave smoothed and shiny, is punctuated with cracked, irregularly shaped outcroppings scattered about randomly, like enormous shriveled raisins spilled from a gigantic hand.

The wild primal scene before me speaks of unimaginable forces that change the landscape, recorded here in sinuous rock ledges snaking seaward. I see the effects of earthquakes, uplifting and displacement from rising and falling sea levels over hundreds of thousands of years. In the tortured, sculpted shapes of the rocky shore, geological time is preserved in a bas relief to be read like a Greek frieze on the Parthenon.

Most of the year several feet of sand covers the twisted rocks, disguising their primeval contortions and the history they record. The sand will return in the summer when this exposed backbone of beach is once again submerged. Only the most massive rock ribs will then pierce the sand carpet like bones of a giant sea monster half buried in a beach grave.

I descend the steep concrete ramp to the beach and pick my way through piles of driftwood and cobbles until I reach the trail around Pelican Point. There, as a casualty of last night's heavy rain, part of the sandstone bluff has given way, and fallen in sharp jagged pieces across the path. A watermelon sized chunk, cracked off during the storm, exposes a crystalline vein of silica, giving me a glimpse of nature's glitter formed hundreds of thousands of years ago and hidden within the rock until today. The silica flashes tiny sparkles of light as I walk past and I wonder if my eyes are the first to record its entry into sunlight and air.

Further on, past the beach cottages at Crystal Cove, huge chunks of coquina rock from a layer high in the bluff above, have broken off and tumbled down onto the beach below. Once part of an ancient sea bottom, the coquina is now a jumble of fossilized sea shells cemented together in a hard sand matrix. I pick up a small piece and run my finger tips over edges of embedded shells. They are packed tightly, overlapping, one on top of another. Each is a fossil, a remainder of a once living creature that existed in the sea before modern man came into being. Most are bleached white with time, but a few retain some of their natural colors. Even after thousands of years, bits of soft pink and tawny beige peek out from the white rock.

As I look up at the coquina layer embedded high above me in the sandstone cliff, I think about the torturous journey that brought it full circle. Beginning at the bottom of the sea as the earth shuddered and shook, the layer of shells was lifted from the ancient seabed and left high in the land mass where time and pressure hardened it into stone.

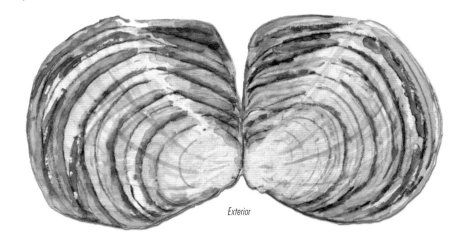

Exterior

This attractive pinkish shell is a Bark Semele, *Semele decisa,* and may be found from San Pedro, California to Mexico. At 4-5 inches it is one of the larger mollusks.

Now softer material beneath it has eroded causing the coquina to break and fall back to the beach in irregular chunks. These tectonic forces raising the land and lowering the sea are beyond my comprehension. Even though I have experienced several strong earthquakes, my consciousness struggles to imagine earth's power bringing about the cataclysmic changes I see in evidence here.

I sit on one of the large coquina slabs still thinking about massive forces shaping the landscape, when my thoughts shift to the subtle and complex forces shaping a life. We are all subject to influences we don't plan on, but which impact how our lives develop. For me, marriage and job opportunities dictated where to live and how. Because of the person I married and the company he worked for, I moved from the Midwest to California, where I found this beach that gives me so much.

Living in California means always the chance a major earthquake may strike without warning and with disastrous effects. I plan my life and prepare for the future, but forever lurking out of sight are elements that can disrupt my plans and reshape me. Even on a small scale, a broken leg or injured back causes major adjustments in routine and ability. Life threatening illnesses are discovered with shock and take precedence over everything else, ruling supreme during periods of treatment. As one fortunate enough to recover from cancer, I recognize I am forever changed in my outlook on life. Influences out of my control may also turn out to be blessings in disguise as they compel me to grow and meet challenges.

As the coquina layer was changed from a collection of living creatures into solid fossilized rock, it may, under the right conditions and over many more thousands of years, further change into limestone or marble. Nature begins with one material, but over time transforms it into another. As heat, pressure and eons change limestone to marble, stress and pressure change

people, leaving them better or worse. Each of us, becomes something related to, but different from our beginnings. The forces operating upon us may not be of our choosing, but how we react to them and what we become because of them are within our control. Unlike the rocks and coquina, we have a choice.

A few years back, the effects of change were evidenced in another fossil unearthed near Crystal Cove. A six foot long ancient tuna skeleton embedded in rock took men with jack hammers to retrieve it. Able to work only at low tide while they dodged the surf, the giant fish skeleton was edged up the beach a few feet at a time, during the backwash of receding waves. This massive block holding fossilized remains of ancient sea life is only one of the multitude in Orange County, where marine mammals and sea life endure in a fossil record diverse in both species and geologic time.

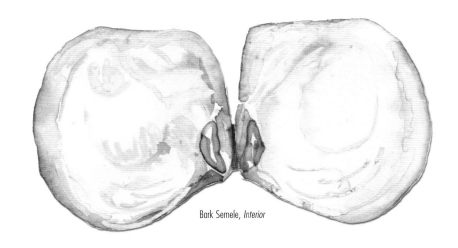

Bark Semele, *Interior*

113

My first experience with fossils took place in a makeshift laboratory at a vacant elementary school, where I was given the task of chipping a whale ulna (fin bone corresponding to our arm bone) out of its matrix. I spent a day in the lab every week absorbed in the slow process of uncovering a remnant of prehistoric life from unknown thousands, perhaps millions of years ago. As I learned more and more about fossils my world expanded with an awareness that helped me see beyond ordinary rocks and to recognize an unusual shape among the boulders one morning on my beachwalk. When I looked closer, my heart skipped a beat, because there, staring at me out of the stone was the end section of a very large vertebra. Later identification proved it to be part of the backbone of a whale who roamed the seas long before man came into being.

Since then, I have gone on to dig dinosaur bones in Colorado and fossil plant material in Wyoming. But I will always treasure most, that first discovery made alone on Horse Beach not far from the coquina rocks that speak to me of time and change and endurance.

It is the antiquity of rocks and fossils that impresses me, that stays glued in my memory and places my life in perspective. I realize I am but a tiny speck of matter existing for less then a fraction of a second in geologic time. Nevertheless, the brevity of my life is not diminished by comparison to the duration of the rocks. My life is of great importance to me and those around me. I am not insignificant. What I do, what I say, what I become, has value. I am a part of the grand scheme of things, just as each tiny shell is necessary to make the layer of coquina.

The fossils remind me, as do the rocks, my fraction of a second on this earth counts. My time need not be remembered or revered; each moment needs only to be as good as I can make it. However small my influence, it will leave a legacy. The coquina rocks whisper their wisdom, I need only listen.

Coquina is rock composed of shells naturally cemented together, often in a sandstone base. This kind of rock began as lake or ocean bottom.

Textures
the magnificent plan

"The best remedy for those who are afraid, lonely or unhappy is to go outside somewhere where they can be quiet, alone with the heavens, nature and God. Because only then does one feel that all is as it should be ... amidst the simple beauty of nature."

Anne Frank, diary entry for February 23, 1944

It is late March. As the coastal terrace springs to life with fresh green leaves sprouting on dry winter stalks, the beach below retains its winter berm, a narrow two-to-four foot high shelf recording the height of the summer strand. Seaward from the berm, storm waves have removed most of the thick, sand blanket, exposing the skeletal body of the rocky shore. Sharp, tilted rocks and twisted outcroppings jut skyward from bands of stone extending along the tide line. These secret, hidden under body parts of the beach are revealed only for a short time in years when severe storms scrape away extra large amounts of sand. Today the beach is stretched out naked, its layers removed, its flesh and bones exposed.

I am drawn to the water's edge where I see a tumble of weathered, wave-sanded ledges. A scattering of pockmarked boulders displays decorative patterns of concentric white rings against black stone. The horizontal shelf extending from the shore is split with a myriad of cracks reminding me of cobble stones. In contrast, here and there gouged out bowls retain a soup of watery sand. These still, mirrored pools reflect mottled blue and gray sky. Today the beach is a study of textures, varied and subtle in their differences.

As I look closely at the ordinary rocks around me, I see banding and color variations I never before noticed. An elongated boulder with an eroded surface shows alternating light and dark ruffled bands. Where each tier of stone terminates into the beach, a small rivulet of sea water creates a wash into the sand extending the influence of the slab. Nearby, other large rock fragments lie half-buried, thrusting their mass upward at odd angles. Sienna, blue-gray and rust, marbled together decorate a stone rib resting slightly askew, off balance. Its layers, each a tiny fraction of an inch thick, smoothed and defined by erosion, confront me with thousands of years of ocean bottom melded together, a record of time condensed in a monument of ancientness.

The beach this morning takes me beyond sand and water and gives me a small glimpse of my planet's grandeur. I realize I am looking at major land formations in miniature. Jagged western mountains, canyons of the mighty Colorado River, eroded Utah red rock, mirrored mountain lakes, sand covered deserts, all are scaled down to playhouse size and I, the giant child, stand above them. I can step over or on top of a mountain peak, reroute Yosemite falls with my hand or dig a meteor crater.

Though I think of myself as both tiny and limited, I know I am also part of a great and magnificent plan replete with sublime textures. This morning's beach forces me to look at myself and think about my own personal textures. Just as layers of ancient sea bottom make up the rocks at my feet, layer upon layer of small moments texture my day. Activities and events fold over one another and meld together like bright rays of sunshine filtering through glistening ocean spray. Family and friends advance and recede into my life like beach tides, leaving behind the flotsam and jetsam created by human relationships.

Inspiration for dealing with my own emotions, comes from watching the ocean as a master chameleon of changing textures. Wild whitecapped waves, huge swells with dark shadows and brilliant sparkling reflections on calm, blue-green water, create a hypnotic changing vista. The constant movement and contrast command my attention. I relate the ocean's moods to my own feelings that vary daily as a variety of personal textures enlivens and excites my spirit. But dealing with textures that are negative

Textured brown seaweed, actually brown alga, often washes onto the beach in small, round, wrinkled clumps. When I first began seeing the strange-looking clumps, I had no idea it was seaweed.

takes conscious thought. My car gets scratched, an appointment makes me wait, or I lose something important. If I think of these minor nuisances as textures contributing color to my life, instead of viewing them as trauma, then I have learned something worthwhile. Major events like joyous celebrations or calamities are beyond texture and must be dealt with on another level.

The sand I walk on this morning, disturbed and studded with yesterday's footprints shows me a texture different from the flat, damp, wave-smoothed surface at the water's edge. It is all the same material, but external forces shape it into different patterns. I am like the sand. I change according to events which affect me. Thinking about this, I pause and sit quietly for a moment smoothing away yesterday's footprints with my hands. As I change the texture of the beach, I wish it were always this easy to change some of yesterday's emotional prints and smooth away hurts and bad feelings.

Shifting from the sand to the sky, I watch clouds ooze from one shapeless mass to another between windows of blue. Cotton puffs dissolve, giving way to blinding light creating infinite shapes fading to muted pink and lavender. I am learning to see the textural value of subtle, shifting blues and grays, as well as the traditionally recognized screaming red-orange, purple-mauve sunset. I am reminded to take nothing for granted, but to look and record the beauty of each moment.

The exposed rocks I admire this morning may tomorrow be once again concealed under a quilt of sand. Subtle changes have messages that speak both of infinity and the immediate present. So I must take advantage of today to see and enjoy their natural textures and record them as a part of my consciousness, or I will have lost an opportunity along with a small portion of myself.

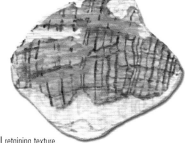

Shell remnants, beach smoothed but still retaining texture.

117

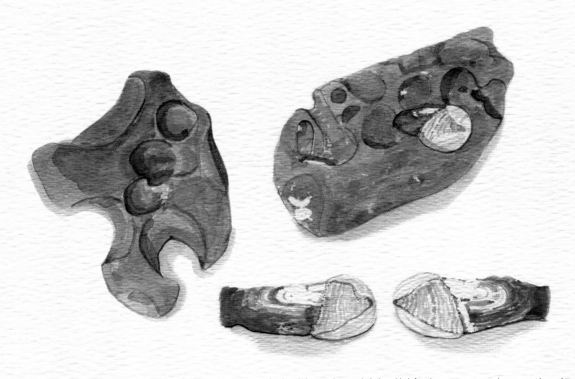

Common Piddock, *Penitella penita*. This boring clam, uses a rough rasplike anterior end to bore holes in rocks into which the piddock fits, thus creating many rock sections with round impressions. My husband wouldn't believe me when I first told him about Piddock Clams boring into rocks. It took a textbook to convince him.

Secret Garden

peace is in the doing

"All things share the same breath - the beast, the tree, the man...
the air shares its spirit with all the life it supports."
Chief Seattle

It's Saturday and I'm not going to the beach. Instead, I look forward to spending the day in my secret garden. In the same way the beach provides a place to go for discovery and renewal, my garden is a sanctuary nourishing me with scents, colors and surprises created by growing plants. Under the trees, amidst the greenery, I can stay at home and still be far away in spirit. It suits me very well for a different kind of beachwalk.

My garden is not one of picket fences, roses and climbing sweet peas. It is, instead, a secret place, a treed and sheltered strip of land sloping gently down from the house to the street below. Spring blooming yellow Acacia trees and white blossoming Myoporums shade the terraced enclosure and conceal most of the meandering paths. Bushes and foliage block views from the street and everywhere, a canopy of green flourishes overhead. When the intense midday sun beats down on black asphalt pavement and concrete sidewalks, it is cool and pleasant in the canopied soft shade of this hidden spot. People walk past on the street and I hear them, but I see them only as brief flashes of color through openings in my leafy wall. It is easy for me to be so far removed in my mind from the street and the house I am truly in another world, a secluded almost magical place, where dreams and play are welcome companions.

The garden grew from an impenetrable jungle of overgrown brush when we moved into this house, to a series of cleared areas for sculpture and homemade art. It is a garden of bits and pieces. Broken gray slate from our original house patio covers the treads on one set of steps. Red terra cotta tiles from our old kitchen pave the floor of a sculpture niche. The marble hearth that once graced the living room is now a moss covered garden bench next to a plaster Corinthian column rescued from a neighbor's trash.

Partially hidden nooks hold small surprises, a garden nymph surrounded by Fortnight Lilies, sea-rounded beach stones from my many beachwalks, and driftwood nesting under leggy geraniums straining to bloom in the shade. Everywhere there are remnants from the sea. An old fashioned, round cork lifesaver encircles a cluster of wild flowers. A fat, braided ship's rope brought up from the beach by one of my grandsons and a wire sculpture constructed from storm dislodged lobster traps all serve as reminders this is a seaside garden where beach objects are as at home as a bed of flowers.

While my garden was not originally meant as a tribute to the ocean, somehow, mementos of times spent near the water crept into corners and nooks, cementing the land and sea together. My beach totems made from colorful lobster buoys strung upright on metal rebar are not only symbolic of my many years of walking the beach, they also give focus to the intent of the garden and confirm its status as a sanctuary perched on land, but influenced by the sea. On a quiet afternoon, sitting in my garden and looking out at the waves and sailboats, I feel the link in the chain between land and water. I picture the ground under my feet merging into the ocean, which throws its essence into salty sea air and blue sky that returns to touch the land. All is connected and flowing in one eternal circle.

Sometimes I give myself the gift of a whole day to work in my garden, although I never work there, I only play. No matter how hard I dig, bend, pull, or lift, I am happy. My mind is free and becomes a receptacle attracting the slightest seed of a new thought. I think I am concentrating on creating a special outdoor vignette with pruning, weeding and rearranging driftwood, but the physical work I do cannot occupy my mind, so ideas sprout like new plants and grow into maturity while my hands rearrange the landscape.

I am ever hopeful that when I leave the garden at the end of the day, it will be perfect, just as I want it. And just as I am ever hopeful, I am always disappointed. As soon as the Yucatan steps (so named because they are rather steep with narrow treads like the Chichen Itza and Uxmal pyramids in the Yucatan) are freed of the continuously advancing ivy and persistent mint, I find the path to the beach totems sprouting new weeds and overhead tree growth so dense it forces me to duck my head as I walk along the path. How naive I am to think in static terms of things that are meant to be growing and changing.

On my beachwalks, I expect change. I look forward to each day's difference and appreciate its unique characteristics. But because I am creating my garden, I expect it to stay the way I design it. And so it continues to defy me with wayward growth I can't control. It has taken me a long time to realize I must think of it in the same way I view the beach. The basic structure remains constant, but details are never the same and it is details, that make it all so interesting.

Through the years I see seasonal patterns and changes in both my garden and the beach. I've learned that both are a process more than a result. I now understand that if I could make my garden perfect once and for all and it stayed that way, I would very soon grow bored and tired of it. Just as if my beachwalks were the same every day, I would soon become disinterested. It is the process of growth and discovery which is stimulating and challenging.

My garden and my beachwalks are both mini versions of my life, a constant striving for specific achievements that will be satisfying to me. But as each goal is realized, a replacement pops up to fill the void. I weed and trim and sow one garden area while another is busy maturing and going to seed. I devote my time to a project pushing all others aside and then it is finished and over. I search through piles of beach cobbles for a perfect shell specimen one day, the next they are all gone and the beach is rearranged with piles of seaweed where before there were shells and pebbles. I think, how can I have inner peace when I'm constantly striving? I am learning that peace is in the doing. Peace comes through enjoying the process of experiencing and learning. The final result matters less than the challenge and process of getting there.

I call these styrofoam floats my beach totems because they represent so many facets of my beach experience. Winds and tides loosen them from the lobster traps they mark and often they end up on shore.

121

So today, I happily clip and prune and transplant knowing none of it will stay the way I leave it, but all of it will result in pleasant discoveries later, as each plant follows its own pattern of growth, flowering, seeding, death and rebirth. Its cycle, like the tides on the beach, continues and I am merely an observer who looks on with wonder.

I love the opportunistic ways of Field Bind-weed, *Convolvulus arvensis*. As an alien, it grows in disturbed places and climbs on other plants. It may be considered a weed, but it also can be very pretty. Another name is Wild Morning Glory.

California Encelia is a woody shrub that grows profusely on the coastal terrace and cliff-sides of Crystal Cove State Park. Its yellow flowers appear in the spring to decorate the hills.

Petrified Wood
bridge to the ancient

"What nature delivers us is never stale. Because what nature creates has eternity in it."

Isaac Bashevis Singer

While I usually take my beachwalk with no plan in mind, today I want to check on a beach discovery from the past. I head down coast towards Pelican Point wondering if the ocean will reveal one of its mysteries or hide it from me under a veil of sand. The tide, on its way out, leaves exposed layers of cracked rock and splintered stone shelves with tiny rivulets of water draining seaward. Stepping from one gray boulder to another, I finally reach my destination, a large, flat, stone slab lying amidst a jumble of similar rocks resting on the coastal shelf at Pelican Point. Embedded in the slab is a petrified tree trunk. I discovered it many years ago while walking near the water's edge at low tide. The flat, three by five foot stone caught my attention because of its unusual surface pattern. When I looked closely, I realized I was viewing the inner section of an ancient tree trunk, once growing on land, but now fossilized wood encased in a rocky tomb. It was as if the tree had been sliced in half lengthwise, laying bare the inner structure of the wood half submerged in a casket of concrete.

Glacial Whelk

Spiny Trophon

I had no idea how many thousands or hundreds of thousands of years old it might be, but I was so excited I reported my find to the Crystal Cove Park rangers thinking they might want to remove it to the visitor center for display. I was disappointed when they indicated leaving the piece in place was their policy. That was over fifteen years ago and the slab remains where I first spotted it. I often check on it as I pass by on my beachwalk. It lies uncovered mostly in the winter when storm waves scrub the beach carrying tons of sand out to sea. In the summer, the rock with its petrified prize is usually buried in the beach sands so I can only guess at its exact position. Other times, angry waves smash over and around it making it impossible for me to get anywhere close.

Today, I stand next to the rock and run my fingers along the outline of the embedded tree. The clear, crisp, obvious wood features that first caught my attention have become muted, less distinct. Now it is so weathered, smoothed by water and sand and waves, I can barely make out the grain of the wood that once was so predominant.

Gem Rock Shell

Seeing how quickly this fossilized wood is being altered by beach conditions, I realize it is softer than other petrified wood I've seen, so it is probably also younger. Knowing how driftwood collects on the beach after storms and how it gets moved and buried by waves and changes in sand levels, I can picture how this petrified tree trunk came into being. But the actual process of changing from wood to stone still amazes me. To become fossilized or petrified, a piece of wood must be buried and subjected to great pressures and/or heat. If conditions are right, its molecules of wood will slowly be replaced with the same minerals that make up rocks. So the structure of the wood remains, but the material it is made of is changed.

How old is this chunk of petrified wood and rock. How many thousands or millions of years did it take for the tree trunk lying in the sand at Pelican Point to turn to stone? Was the tree alive and growing fifty to a hundred thousand years ago when ground sloths, saber-toothed tigers and mammoths roamed this area? Or could it have been a part of the landscape over sixty million years ago when dinosaurs ruled the earth?

I will never know its true age, but I do know it is a bridge to the ancient past, a connection I can see, touch and marvel at. Just as the prehistoric scraper tool I found on the bluff top connects me to ancient people, this petrified wood tree trunk connects the beach of today with its geological past. There is more driftwood buried beneath the sand I walk on. It is undergoing some small step in the process of fossilizing and some of it will complete the transformation and pass into the distant future as petrified wood.

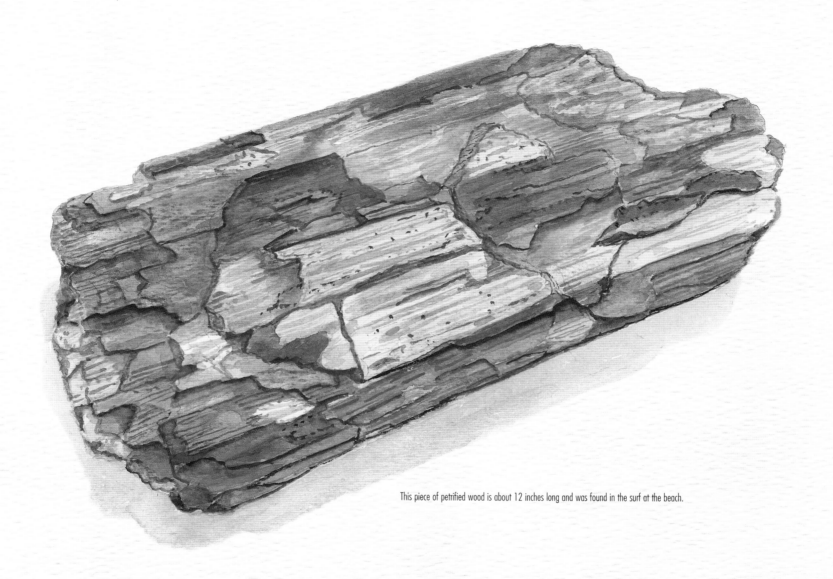

This piece of petrified wood is about 12 inches long and was found in the surf at the beach.

New eyes may gaze at it and wonder about its origin. just as I wonder today. So the cycle continues and each time I check on the state of the petrified tree trunk at Pelican Point, I am a witness to one tiny portion of a natural process eternally at work, preserving the past.

On my way home, as I continue thinking about fossils, I am reminded of another piece of petrified wood I recently found here at the water's edge. On that day I was at the end of my beachwalk heading for the steps, when I noticed a small 4 by 12 inch piece of wood lying alone in a nest of sand near the swash line. Having already passed beyond it, I felt something was not quite right, so I turned back for a second look. Although it appeared to be bleached, gray driftwood, when I picked it up its cold, hard surface and heavy weight confirmed it was really rock. Serendipity had given me another treasure from the beach.

I once found piece of petrified wood on the shore of Big Bear Lake in the San Bernardino Mountains of southern California. On that day I was raking and cleaning up our shore front, getting ready for the summer boating and canoeing season, when once again one of the stones had a different look. As soon as I picked it up I knew it was no ordinary rock, but instead a piece of petrified wood. I'm very curious as to how it came to rest on my lake shore. If petrified wood were a common occurrence in these mountains as it is in parts of Utah and Colorado, I would just accept it without question, but I don't think it is common here.

My beachwalk this morning is satisfying and I feel stimulated. Thoughts aroused from mulling about wood turning to stone, a natural process of preservation, go home with me and sit in my mind like the piece of petrified wood that sits on my coffee table.

Different types of rock shells, some would be found in coquina, rock made up of fossil shells cemented together by nature.

Sand

unique workings of the human spirit

To see the world in a grain of sand
And a Heaven in a wild flower,
Hold infinity in the palm of your hand
And Eternity in an hour!
William Blake

Between the crumbling sandstone bluff and leading edge of a new tide rushing up the sloping shore, a narrow swath of sand remains untouched by incoming waves. This is the path I follow on my beachwalk this morning. Not far away, an elaborate sand castle constructed by yesterday's beach users, still stands firm. It has four corner towers, crenelated walls and a deep moat. A path of small pebbles paves the tiny road leading to a drawbridge of dried kelp. More pebbles are placed atop the outer walls and tiny flags made from bits of dried seaweed wave from each of the four corners. The rounded castle roof is laid with Purple Olive shells in concentric rows and a Wavy Top shell adds a spiral turret to the central tower. Inside the castle wall an arched tunnel bisects the main part of the castle. Very carefully, I insert my hand as far as my elbow to see if it goes all the way through. The tunnel is intact, even though the sand has dried overnight. Here is an idealized world, a simulated version of man's need to create.

Someone spent a lot of time building and adorning this sand structure. I wonder how many people worked on it and whether any were children. The delightful thing is that adults do not hesitate to play in the sand because building sand castles at the beach is acceptable for anyone. We express our dreams in sand. We build a fortress, a fairy tale castle, a lake with bridges, a race car track, a turtle, a dolphin, and it need not be perfect. Anything we make is fine. People who would never consider picking up a pencil to draw a picture don't hesitate for a second when it comes to building with sand.

I'm glad the castle survived the night, but the early morning high tide is only inches away and will soon fill the moat. I wonder if it will all be gone, leveled by advancing waves, when I return this way at the end of my walk. Heading south at a brisk pace to the cottages at Crystal Cove, the brightness of the morning makes me squint. I pull my hat further over my eyes and focus downward away from the low angled, rising sun. Near my feet I notice little raised circles of sand indicating life beneath the surface, so I sit down and dig to see if I can uncover the tunnelers of the beach. Even after I scoop out a fairly large hole, I find nothing. The wet sand from below the surface clings to my hands and stays in a nice high mound as I pat and shape it. The dry surface sand is loose and dribbles through my fingers like rivulets of water.

The simple pleasure I feel playing with the sand leads to digging a bigger hole and building a bigger mound as my thoughts and hands become mesmerized by the flow and feel of tiny grains of quartz against my skin. Sand brings out the child in all of us. It gives

interior

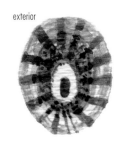
exterior

Volcano Limpet, pink with radiating darker lines from the center hole

Rough Limpet interior

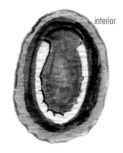
interior

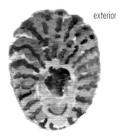
exterior

Owl Limpet with owl-like brown design on the inside

128

us permission to relax, to use our tactile senses and indulge in imaginative play. As I sit smoothing miniature pebbles back and forth for the sheer pleasure of how it feels, I realize the sand is in command. It wills my involvement with its rounded particles. I am soothed like a baby gently patted into sleepiness.

In my research on sand, I find it has some unique properties. Its structure places it in a special category called granular material. One of the unusual ways granular material behaves is to sort itself by size. To be logical I would expect the largest and heaviest pieces to fall downward to the bottom, with the lightest and smallest at the top. Instead, the smallest grains collect in the lower layer with the largest at the top, which is how sand gets its uniformity. Even more strange is that granular materials do not mix over time. Instead, they align themselves into tidy stacks or layers. There is no good explanation for how this happens. It seems to disobey the laws of nature and perhaps this is one of the reasons sand castles are such fun to build. We get to play with a material that has some characteristics not found in common soil. Sand allows us to construct tunnels through mounds that should collapse but don't, put up bridges that shouldn't hold but do, and to form walls that lean without proper supports.

Wet sand is the best building material. Water works almost like glue holding the grains together, so that when making a large pyramid, we would expect the highest point of pressure to be under the top of the mound, but it isn't. It's in a ring around the apex or highest point. Sand somehow distributes its weight unevenly, forming unexpected lines of force that even scientists don't quite understand. Neither do we understand the human spirit, which, also defies every logical explanation known to man. Like the sand, we do not understand it, we can only see it in action or observe its results.

I think parenting is like the sand. It has unknown and unrecognized lines of force with no laws of definition. If there were a scientific formula for being a good parent, most of us would happily follow it. Lacking that, we take actions expecting a certain result and often get one different from what we wanted.

One time when I was exasperated by my five year old son's room with toys and clothes strewn everywhere, in desperation, I finally said, "You have to pick up your toys or you'll get a spanking." He sat for a few long seconds before answering and finally said, "I thought it over and I'll take the spanking." His two older sisters dissolved in spasms of laughter they tried to conceal, and I, who had no intention of spanking him anyway, had to leave the room until I could stop laughing and put a stern look on my face. Then I had to explain to him that I wasn't really giving him a choice, he had to pick up his toys and I had threatened him out of my own frustration. He sighed and reluctantly trudged off to his room, cleaning up just enough to get by.

interior  exterior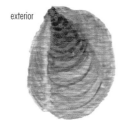

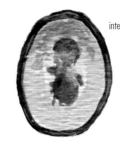

interior 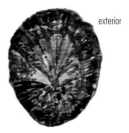 exterior

Slipper Shell, thick with purplish-brown exterior

Rough Limpet exterior

Flie limpet, brown with radical ribs

I was never successful in motivating him to keep his toys and clothes picked up. It wasn't until years later after putting up with a messy roommate in college that he turned into a neat person liking everything in its place. Never could I have predicted a messy roommate would achieve in a few weeks that which I was unable to do in 18 years. It was one of those strange lines of force that operate without our knowledge. In this example and countless other ways, I know my influence upon my children was there, but I certainly can't explain how it worked. It was like the tunnel through a sand castle that logically should cave in, but doesn't, because of the special properties of sand we don't understand. How much less we understand about the uniqueness and individuality of ourselves and those around us.

As I sit digging my heels into the loose granular material of the beach, dribbling it through my fingers, I feel at peace with myself and lulled into contentment. My thoughts today inspired by the sand beneath my feet, help me to know myself a little better. Sandcastle dreams provide an entry into aspects of my human spirit. I am reminded of so much I don't understand and never can. But it doesn't matter, like granular material sorting itself into piles, life gets sorted out whether I understand or not.

I would like to stay and play in this pleasant place, but I realize it is time to go home and begin the rest of my day. After all I was privileged to have the luxury of an early morning walk and some playtime in a really big sand box.

The poet was right, I can ......"see the world in a grain of sand." As I pass by the area where earlier I admired the sand castle, all that remains is a shallow puddle of foamy sea water, a few scattered pebbles and some dried up seaweed.

Sand Dollars, *Dendraster excentricus,* are in the same class, *Echinoidea,* as Sea Urchins. They live only on protected sand flats.

130

Catalina Ghosts
the past shapes the present

"All history is but a romance, unless it is studied as an example."

George Croly

On my way home from the beach, I pause and look back at the stretch of sand and sea behind me, a habit I've developed to impress the special beauty of each day into my permanent memory bank. Through a thin veil of morning mist hovering above the ocean's surface, I catch glimpses of a ship with black sails. I watch as it moves slowly in wispy fog, like a ghost ship, an apparition, an unreal remnant from another time, the days of exploration and Spanish galleons. The black sails, so different from most of today's white or bright colored combinations, stimulate my imagination, summoning up images of pirates and legends of ghost ships sailing into infinity, condemned by some horrible misdeed committed in times past.

I choose a smooth boulder to sit on as I watch the black-sailed ship fade in and out of sight while low lying clouds softly swirl above the waves. Soon weak morning light begins to pierce the clouds and further out, beyond the ship, a long, low, ghostly shape like a gigantic sea serpent slowly takes on definition as it appears to emerge from a steamy sea. It is the island of Santa Catalina, still partially nestled in low clouds and remnants of morning fog. On sunny days, shining white cliffs near its south end and only town, Avalon, are visible across the water. But on this misty morning I can only wait to see if the skies will clear and reveal the illusive island. Meanwhile the black-sailed ship slowly disappears from sight into the pewter gray of sea and mist.

In ancient geologic time Santa Catalina was connected to the continent. I could have walked there from where I now sit thinking about ghost ships and ghostly islands. Through subduction, earthquakes and upheavals, Catalina moved thirty miles seaward from today's coast. And while it is not far away in miles, it seems

Used since ancient times for food and ornaments

years away in time. A Civil War Union Army barracks built in 1864 still stands between two sheltered harbors on a low, narrow neck of land that bisects the island at the Isthmus. The old wooden barracks building now serves as an unusual yacht club where members have their own rooms and maintain the building themselves on scheduled work weekends. At one time my husband and I had a room there and I once shared an evening with the ghost of a Civil War Army Captain, who, I had been told, walked the halls creaking the floorboards at night.

When I first heard stories about a ghostly presence I thought they were quaint and a rather nice touch for the picturesque building whose age and history keep it alive and standing as much as its walls and foundation. As with many old buildings, a dank, musty smell that no amount of fresh air can alter, permeates the rooms, wind rattles glass in old window frames and creaky sounds issue from unknown sources. One night when I was alone in my room with no one else in the building, I heard footsteps in the hallway. The hair on the back of my neck stood on end and goose bumps broke out on my arms. I felt an eerie sensation as I froze in place, listening. The footsteps grew louder as they approached my door and weakened as they receded down the hallway. Then all was quiet.

After I calmed down I wondered if I had actually heard something or only imagined it. How ridiculous, I told myself, to let the power of suggestion affect me so strongly.

Venus Clams are named after the goddess, Venus, for their graceful lines and beauty of color.

132

But about a year later, one of my daughters, unaware of the ghost stories, had the same experience of an eerie presence when she was alone in the building while the rest of the family was still in the kitchen, a separate and newer addition. Finally, even my husband admitted sometimes he felt the building was spooky when other people were not around.

In wondering about the ghost, I think, could it be the Union Army Captain as rumored or perhaps someone else connected with the building? Certainly, it has had its share of occupants, beginning with the first Civil War soldiers, then after a period of abandonment, the Coast Guard during World War II, and finally Hollywood studios cut the large barracks into small rooms for their movie stars while filming on the island. If the ghost is really Clark Gable or Charles Laughton, both of whom stayed there during the early movie making era, I should have opened my door to the hallway and invited him in.

Smooth California Venus Clams, *Chione fluctifraga.*

Long before the barracks was built the flat meadow it rests upon was thought to be the location of a temple built to the God, Chinigchinich, by the Pimugnans, the first known inhabitants of Catalina Island. I've spent hours browsing in the small museum in Avalon where artifacts left by these early people are on display. Soapstone bowls, effigies, flutes, pipes, obsidian blades, shellfish hooks, manos and metates all carry images in my mind of the people they represent. On the ground around the barracks building I have found small, polished pieces of black soapstone, remnants I think, left by these ancient native Americans. Perhaps they have left spirit remnants as well.

One day while hiking around the island, I unexpectedly came upon one of their middens or trash heaps. Black earth turned dark from cooking fires, grease and waste, along with white shell pieces embedded in the dirt were typical signs of a midden. I stopped to look more closely and there, protruding from the blackened earth on the side of the road was a mano, the rounded stone used for grinding acorns into meal. I was really excited to have discovered a midden on my own. Later, on a different hike at the edge of the bay, I came across another Indian trash heap with whole mollusk shells lying about on the surface of a black earth patch. Clams and other shellfish, we know were a major food for these early dwellers. It occurs to me that maybe the ghost of the barracks building is really one of these ancient people, seeking to reclaim ancestral ground.

Another possible ghost source is in Cat Harbor located on the outer or seaward side of the Isthmus. Hidden there are the remains of the Chinese junk, *Ningpo,* once known as the pirate ship, *Kai Tai Foong.* She came to the island under her own sail and was used as a movie set for many years before disintegrating. Now only a few ghostly timbers protrude from the sea bed at low tide. Might there be ghostly spirits from the ship's pirate days still lurking about as well?

Even nature has its version of the ghost of Catalina. Most of the time *Coreopsis gigantea* or Sea Dahlia exists only as a dry dead-looking stalk. But when rains come it bursts in to bloom, covering the steep cliffs overhanging the sea with spectacular yellow bouquets. Truly a ghost flower, it is worthy of its place on a mysterious island that shimmers in sunlight on some mornings and lies buried in the mists on others.

133

As close or as far as an eyelid's blink or a swirl of low fog, Catalina is sometimes a part of my beachwalk experience and sometimes not. It's elusiveness encourages me to wander backward in my mind and connect it with the mythical Avalon of King Arthur, the inspiration for the naming of the town of Avalon on the island. The Arthurian legend itself is unclear and leaves room for mystic stories. Somehow, I think, Catalina as it fades in and out of my view is not only a ghostly island, but with all of its varied and colorful history there must be many ghosts to walk at night.

As I shift my weight on the hard rock where I sit, Santa Catalina disappears entirely from my view and the fog deepens, graying both sea and sky. The ship with black sails is gone, swallowed by the mist and I, too, must leave for another place. I walk home through a gentle sprinkling of rain, thinking about ghost ships and my ghostly experience on a ghost island.

I ask myself, " Do I really believe in ghosts? I don't think so." But I would like to believe in them as remnants of the past cautioning me against becoming too self important in my own time. They are reminders I am here and everything around me is possible only because of all that existed and came before me. The spirits of the past exist in my mind to keep me humble and aware of history's effect upon the present.

Wavy Top Shell, *Astraea undosa*, with Scaly Worm Tubes attached. This shell, faded with time, was found in an Indian midden. It was one of the shellfish used for food.

134

Crystal Cove
caretakers of the beach

"People protect what they love."
Jacques Yves Cousteau

About midway on my walk along the beach towards the southern end of Crystal Cove State Park, I pass a cluster of vintage beach cottages nestled in a wide cove. Fronted by a smooth swath of sand, these forty-six houses, most built over half a century ago are lived in by year 'round residents as well as weekend vacationers. Tucked into the cliff side or perched atop the bluff, they are weathered and worn with the patina of many years of beach life and salt air. As I approach the enclave on a weekday morning, it is quiet and sleepy. Wisps of sweet wood smoke spiral upward from one of the chimneys and the smell of bacon and pancakes overrides the smell of the sea.

There is little resemblance here to Newport Beach or Laguna Beach, the coastal towns just a few miles away on either side. The cottages, hidden from inland civilization, face out to sea forming their own community, separate and apart from the rest of today's world. Any sound of traffic on the coastal road above is muffled by constant thunder of breaking waves. Each cottage is unique with its own decor of weathered decking, worn outdoor chairs, umbrellas, driftwood arrangements, lobster floats and eccentric beach items culled from the high tide line.

The friend I am visiting this morning, has planted a shark garden in her front yard. Curved fins of surfboard skegs partially buried

in the sand circle their hidden prey. On a level above the prowling sharks, twisted gray driftwood leans against pots of red geranums leading to her front door, where massive honeysuckle and oleander bushes obscure a view of the house from the beach and protect it from buffeting offshore winds.

As we sit and sip our coffee on her deck built of driftwood planks held together with hand-forged spikes, remnants reclaimed from the sea after a storm, I am reminded of the gentle affection and nurturing attention so many Crystal Cove residents have for this special place and the reverence they hold for the sea life around them. Living here full or part-time is multigenerational for many and the heart's home for most.

In the mid 1940's my friend's first experiences here occurred while staying with her grandmother from whom she learned to swim and body surf and soak up the essence of summer. She remembers playing in the burlap sandbag bunkers built on the bluff top as a place to watch for submarines during World War II. Over half a century later, the bunkers are long gone, but she still braves the cold water to swim nearly every morning of the year. "It makes the day go better," she says modestly, while admitting she is sometimes leery to be alone in the big surf when it is especially violent. She remembers swimming out into the path of a pod of dolphins, treading water as they approached. About fifteen feet away they looked at her facing them, disappeared beneath her dangling legs and resurfaced behind her with a whoosh sound of expelled breath. She and the dolphins had communicated in some subtle way and the experience left her with a heightened respect for the presence of wild animals in their natural environment.

Limpet and Hornshark's egg case known as a "Mermaid's Purse." These egg cases wash onto the beach after the shark's egg hatches.

Sea fans and shells: Venus clams and small scallop along with what I call "skeleton branches."

We go inside for another cup of coffee and a look at her collection of beach oddities. The cottage is small and cozy, an eclectic mix of treasures, remembrances and favorite things. We share our self-taught knowledge as we fondle and discuss stiff, curved, black squid beaks, small white coral clumps resembling old-fashioned starched doilies, sea lion whiskers, an elephant seal tooth and fossilized turitella shells from Morro Canyon across the highway, each item lovingly displayed on a bureau top.

Shark egg cases, commonly known as mermaid's purses capture our attention, and we compare notes on two varieties. The spiral form belongs to a Hornshark and the rectangular one is from a skate. These small leather-like pockets wash up on the beach after tiny babies have hatched from eggs inside. The first time I found one buried in a clump of seaweed, I carried it home and spent hours searching my books before I was able to identify it.

I pick up a small triangular arrangement of calcareous plates from a sea urchin's mouth and she reminds me that it, too, has an interesting common name. It is called Aristotle's Lantern because of its small cage-like shape. Together we unsuccessfully search her natural history books trying to identify a black, tree-shaped branch, which reminds me of a sea fan, but neither of us knows its name. The more we talk, the more I renew my own curiosity and desire to know about these offerings left on the beach by ocean waves.

The families of Crystal Cove live daily with the sand and the sea that I experience only during the time I am on my beachwalks. While some Cove residents are picture window people and enjoy the ocean from a safe distance, others inhale its very essence. They notice little things, wiggly lines in the sand made by grunion as they find their way back to water after laying salmon-colored eggs in small sand pockets during high tide, the jewel-like quality of wet sand as it sparkles like diamonds in the morning sun, a piece of driftwood where Carpenter Bees have taken up residence, a fragment of neatly written sign with just enough letters remaining to spell out "sportation." The richness and variety of beach environment here for those who really look and really see, is endless. The smallest of things, a half inch long Coffee Bean shell, can be a treasure, a huge wave an awesome sight. Like life, the beach is as interesting as we make it, fascinating or ordinary, the choice is up to us.

I choose to experience the beach with as much knowledge and through as many sensory images as I can find. Others use the beach for an afternoon of pure relaxation and as a retreat. Each purpose fulfills a need. My hope is that we all understand the importance of the natural world and the creatures in it so that we learn it is possible and desirable to live side by side. To conquer or tame nature for our convenience is to forget that each part of it has a purpose. If we kill every bug and insect that bothers us and get rid of every plant that does not please us, we also lose birds and butterflies. If we flood the ocean with our waste, we poison sea life, from zooplankton to whales, and rich sea beds will become sterile.

We are the caretakers of our natural world. Our existence as a species depends upon how we treat the myriad of other species with whom we share this planet.

The caretakers of Crystal Cove are especially good at recognizing the value of the ocean and beach. Whether appreciation has been passed down through generations of those who inhabited Crystal Cove or whether the environment itself demands and instills attention, I do not know. I do know Cove residents have held an important place in environmental caretaking for many years. Plans are in place to evict the current Cove dwellers and use the cottages for overnight rentals, group retreats, park support and perhaps even a new resort hotel. When the Cove residents are gone, life will continue, but a great void will be left. The beach will be used and enjoyed by many, but it will not have the gentle attention keeping it so natural and so loved for so long. Choices are hard. To know the best use and preservation of a wildlife area is difficult at best and nearly always a compromise.

I leave my friend's cottage and pick up a gray and white gull feather as I trudge towards home. The sun is just beginning to peek through low morning clouds and by the time I reach my house, it is perfect weather for breakfast outside and the morning newspaper, where the troubles of the world assault my being and try my reason. But like my friend's morning swim, my beachwalk "makes the day go better."

Purple Olive Shells were used for bead making by Native Americans.

139

Young Giant Rock Scallops look quite different from the adults. It took some research to connect the small, colorful, fragile specimens with the heavy purple-hinged older shell.

Sunset

moving on

*"Though we travel the world over to find the beautiful,
we must carry it with us or we find it not."*

Ralph Waldo Emerson

Flaming red, magenta and tangerine swirl into violet and mauve as a golden ball slides lower in the afternoon sky, then slips gently over the horizon into the sea. It is sunset, day's end. It is the sunset of my beachwalks, the end of my beach experience. No more will I wander along the shore, the tangy scent of salt water in my nostrils, the sound of pounding surf in my ears. I never thought I'd leave our comfortable spot on the southern California coast; it was here I watched over migrating whales, flocks of seabirds and moody roiling waves from every room in the house. But things change. Discoveries open doors. New horizons beckon. An ad in the newspaper led to an intriguing ranch in the desert. My husband and I had to decide whether we would stay in a spot we loved, closing our eyes to new opportunity or if we would embrace a stimulating challenge. We chose to step through an opened door into a beckoning new world, even though it meant leaving behind all we had loved before.

Our new home in California's Coachella Valley, a two hour drive from the sea coast of Corona del Mar, is not the end of the earth, but it is for us the end of a lifestyle. No more foggy, misty mornings with droplets of moisture collecting on my face as I crossed the golf course and descended wooden stairs to the sand where I spent the early morning searching for surprises left by the evening's tide. Instead I now awaken to bright blue sky and warm dry air as I set off down the gravel driveway to collect the morning newspaper from our mailbox about half a mile away. I am alone except for my dog, the jackrabbits he feels obligated to chase and thorny desert shrubs. Beneath my feet, beach sand is replaced with desert sand. It is a new life, I have new discoveries to make and a new book to write about my desert walks.

I am happy with our choice to move and stimulated by our new environment. While I miss my friends at the beach, I am excited and eager to plunge into the world of prickly pear cactus, creosote bushes and sand dunes. This wave of my life has tossed me ashore onto an enchanted desert isle. Just as each day ends and another begins, the sun having set on my beach wanderings rises anew on a desert landscape.

Now my morning begins with pale pinks and soft yellows emerging slowly from behind a horizon of undulating mountain peaks until at last a burst of brilliance illuminates a cloudless sapphire sky. The wonder of it feeds my heart and bestows a new vocabulary on my journal pages. Life's adventure continues...

142

Sunset with Catalina Island on horizon and Newport Beach harbor breakwaters — the view from my window.

143